DATE DUE

~~MR 2 8~~			
~~MY 18 '99~~			
~~MY 4 '00~~			
~~JE 7 02~~			
~~MY 19 03~~			
~~JE 9 '03~~			
~~DE 1 03~~			
~~DE 17 '04~~			

AMERICA'S
HEALTH CARE
CRISIS

AMERICA'S

CRISIS

WHO'S RESPONSIBLE?

❧

BY NANCY LEVITIN

An Impact Book
FRANKLIN WATTS
New York   Chicago   London   Toronto   Sydney

D JAKE

Library of Congress Cataloging-in-Publication Data

Levitin, Nancy.
America's health care crisis / Nancy Levitin.
p. cm. — (Impact book)
Includes bibliographical references and index.
ISBN 0-531-11187-3
1. Medical care, Cost of — United States. 2. Medical economics — United
States. 3. Medical policy — United States. 4. Insurance, Health —
United States. [1. Medical care, Cost of.] I. Title. II. Series.
RA410.53.L478 1994
338.4'33621'0973—dc20
94–15523 CIP AC

CONTENTS

AMERICA'S
HEALTH CARE
CRISIS

Chapter One

A SYSTEM
IN CRISIS

INTRODUCTION TO AMERICA'S
HEALTH CARE CRISIS

*J*ackie, a first-grader in Pittsburgh, was having trouble in school. She could not follow simple directions, was unable to learn how to speak clearly, and did not play with other children. The school nurse discovered that Jackie had mild hearing loss as a result of untreated ear infections.

Bob Black is a fifty-year-old computer technician. He and his family were covered under health insurance provided by Bob's employer. During the recession Bob was notified that he would no longer be receiving health coverage through work. When Bob started shopping for health insurance on his own he found that no insurer was willing to cover him because he had been diagnosed with prostate cancer two years earlier.

Lori is pregnant with her second child. She is in the fifth month of her pregnancy and still has not seen a doctor. Lori already has a two-year-old son named Sean. Sean weighed only three pounds at birth and now suffers from seizures and hyperactivity. Lori received no prenatal care during her first pregnancy either.

Many believe that the U.S. health care system is in a state of crisis. Statistics tell the sad story of the following:

...costs that are spiraling out of control:
- Americans spent $23,000 per second on medical care, more than $2 billion per day, and about $733 billion per year on medical care in 1991.[1]
- The United States spent more than 14 percent of its gross national product (GNP) on medical costs in 1992, more than education and defense spending combined.[2]
- The average American family paid about $4,000 a year for health coverage in 1990.[3]
- Medical expenses are the major cause of personal bankruptcy.[4]
- A patient hospitalized in 1991 paid about $3.7 for a single Bufferin aspirin.[5]

...millions of Americans who cannot afford basic health care:

- At any given time roughly 37 millionAmericans, or about 1 out of 9, have no insurance at all.[6]
- Only 40 percent of low-income Americans receive *Medicaid* (public medical assistance for the poor).[7]
- The typical beneficiary of *Medicare* (public insurance for the elderly and disabled) spends over 15 percent of her annual income on medical care.[8]

...quality of health care that often falls short of the expenditure:

- Nineteen other developed countries have a lower infant mortality rate (deaths before one year of age) than does the United States.[9] Twice as many babies die during the first year of life in the U.S. than in Japan.[10]

•At least one out of four American children do not receive proper immunizations. The immunization rate in Bangladesh is higher than the rate in Atlanta, Georgia.[11]

•There are almost twenty times more cases of measles today than there were in 1983.[12]

•In America, a premature baby is born every three minutes (often because the mother had no prenatal care).[13]

•Thirty-seven other countries beat America's death rate among women with cancer.[14]

•Total health care spending in the United States will easily top $1 trillion in 1994.[15]

•The number of uninsured people will increase to 40 million by the year 2000.[16]

How has America's health care system reached such a critical state? Who or what is responsible for causing the current crisis?

Is the insurance industry to blame? Critics charge insurers with driving up health care costs by encouraging doctors to set high fees, encouraging hospitals to expand needlessly, failing to cover medical services that save money in the long run, and committing a range of other wrongdoings.

Or is greed of doctors the cause of this country's desperate situation? The lust for money, in the view of many, leads doctors to charge outrageously high fees, perform unnecessary medical procedures, and commit fraud on the health care system.

Should the blame fall on the legal profession? Some accuse lawyers of sending health care costs through the roof by urging disgruntled patients to sue their doctors for malpractice. Fear of malpractice suits, in turn, leads doctors to overtreat their patients and purchase pricey malpractice insurance policies. Patients end up paying for the unnecessary care and insurance premiums in the form of higher medical bills.

Is the cause of the problem the waste and inefficiency that plague the nation's health care system? Examples of these problems are hospitals not filled to capacity; overpurchasing of expensive, state-of-the-art medical equipment; and valuable time and money lost administering over a thousand different health insurance programs.

Do advances in medical technology also share responsibility for rising health care costs? Sophisticated and costly new medical equipment is often overused. Doctors can now keep patients alive longer, often at a cost of thousands of dollars a day.

The chapters that follow examine these possible causes of the health care crisis and others. Proposals for reforming the health care system are discussed throughout the book. Two of the most popular reform proposals, single-payer health insurance and managed competition, are covered in depth in the final two chapters.

Chapter Two

THE INSURANCE GAME

HAVE INSURANCE COMPANIES PLAYED A ROLE IN CAUSING THE HEALTH CARE CRISIS?

*E*veryone hates paying hundreds of dollars to the insurance company month after month, knowing they may never see a penny of the money again, but most people have a justifiable fear of going without insurance. Insurance is supposed to be life's great safety net. When crisis strikes, and expenses mount, insurance is there to foot the bill. People pay their health insurance premiums so they can sleep at night knowing insurance will pay their medical bills if they get hit by a car in the morning.

With the cost of health care as high as it is, one serious illness or injury can financially wipe out just about anyone, even the very wealthy. Going uninsured, in other words, makes tightrope walking without a net look safe.

Despite the invaluable role insurance companies play protecting the people they insure from financial ruin, the insurance industry has been roundly criticized for contributing to the health care crisis in a number of significant ways. Are these charges valid, or has the unpopular insurance industry just become an easy target of critics?

Most Americans use some type of health insurance to pay their medical bills. Patients only dip into their pockets to pay 5 cents of every dollar of hospital services they use, and only 21 cents of every dollar of other medical services they receive.[1] Private insurance carriers and federal and state governments pay most of the rest of the nation's health care tab.

The widespread use of insurance has been blamed for making Americans irresponsible health care consumers. People are not careful about how much they spend on their medical care because they use so little of their own money to pay their medical bills. According to one study, families that paid more of their own medical bills (the first $1,000 a year) spent 40 percent less on their medical care than the families with full insurance coverage. Yet there was almost no difference between the health of the two groups![2]

Just think about the differences between health care consumers and supermarket shoppers. Supermarket shoppers often clip coupons to get 25 cents off for a roll of aluminum foil, or try to save 15 cents on their orange juice by comparing the prices of Tropicana and Minute Maid. They are concerned about the size of their grocery bills because they know when they get to the cashier they will have to take out their wallets, and pay for the groceries.

Health care consumers are an entirely different breed of shopper. A patient looking for a new doctor will ask where the doctor was trained before asking what the doctor charges for an office visit. A patient shopping for a hospital to enter for gallbladder surgery will ask how many gallbladder operations the hospital performs each year before asking how much the operation costs.

The difference in shopping strategies is understandable. Whereas for the supermarket shopper, money is at stake, the health care consumer's health is at stake. In addition, someone else (an insurance company or government agency) will probably pay the health care consumer's bills.

Hospital patients have traditionally been the least careful shoppers of all. This is because they rarely saw their hospital bills. The bills were sent directly from the hospital's billing office to the patient's insurance carrier. This made it very easy for hospitals to jack up their prices. Patients rarely noticed or cared.

This situation is starting to change as patients are being forced to pay a larger share of their hospital bills. People who got insurance coverage through work used to enjoy 100 percent coverage of their hospital expenses. No longer. More and more employers are requiring their employees to make a co-payment. The co-payment is the amount of each medical bill the insured patient must pay.

For example, many employers now cover their workers for only 80 percent of all hospital expenses, while the worker is responsible for a 20 percent co-payment. An employee who racks up a $50,000 hospital bill, for example, will be covered for only $40,000 (80 percent of $50,000). The employee has to pay a $10,000 co-payment. When it comes to hospital care, even the co-payment can reach into the tens of thousands of dollars.

Reviewing a hospital bill to check the accuracy of a co-payment charge is not easy. The standard hospital bill is divided into a few broad categories, such as nursing, laboratory fees, and radiology. The only way a patient can get any real information about what he or she is paying for is to request an itemized statement. The typical itemized statement is dozens of pages long, with lists of mysterious coded entries like "hip-uni 2 die" and "PT-PTT."

Huh?

Notations such as these mean nothing to the average patient who doesn't have an advanced degree in hospital administration. Why do hospitals make their bills impossible for patients to read? Is there a method to the hospital madness?

Maybe. Hospitals certainly have a financial interest in keeping their bills as confusing as possible.

Ninety-nine percent of all hospital bills have been found to include overcharges.[3] These overcharges go undetected as long as patients can't decode their bills. The average hospital bill contains almost $1,400 worth of unnecessary charges.[4] The fewer unnecessary charges patients find, the more money hospitals can collect.

With patients unable to decipher their hospital bills, comparison shopping among hospitals becomes virtually impossible. How can patients intelligently compare the prices and services of different hospitals if they don't know how much they are paying for what? They can't, so hospitals don't have to compete against each other by offering the highest-quality care for the least cost. This allows hospital costs to rise and quality of care to drop.

Why, you might ask, don't the insurance companies who pay most hospital bills hire experts to review the bills for accuracy? Good question.

Insurance companies probably would review hospital bills for accuracy if they could. But they can't. A claims adjuster at the John Hancock Insurance Company, for example, has no way of knowing if Steve, who is insured by John Hancock, requested three or four painkillers after his kidney stones were removed. John Hancock would need this information to determine if Steve was overcharged.

Hospitalized patients are charged for everything from the first aspirin they take in the morning to the extra pillow they request at night. The task of confirming every entry on each page of thousands of lengthy itemized hospital statements is beyond most insurers. Instead the insurers raise their premiums to cover the overcharges.

Most people get health insurance as a benefit of

their employment.[5] Employers started offering their workers health insurance during World War II. With 12 million working-age men serving in the armed forces, there was a smaller pool of able-bodied men looking for employment, and companies had to compete with each other for the limited number of available workers. Wartime wage restrictions prohibited employers from offering their workers more money, so employers began to offer fringe benefits. One of the most popular fringe benefits was free health insurance.

Health insurance continues to be a favorite employment benefit, because health benefits for workers are tax free. Wages are not tax free. A worker who earns $2,000 in wages must pay $600 to $1,000 to the federal, state, and local governments in taxes. The worker would get to take home only $1,000 to $1,400 of the $2,000. But if that same worker receives $2,000 worth of health insurance coverage, the worker would actually get to keep something that was worth $2,000.

The fear of losing health insurance keeps many Americans in jobs they otherwise would leave. Three out of ten people stay in jobs because of concerns about their health coverage.[6] The reluctance to leave a job with good health benefits is commonly known as job lock.

Companies have started to complain that the skyrocketing cost of health insurance is driving them out of business. In 1993 Xerox Corporation spent an average of $6322 insuring each of its employees.[7] Approximately $993 of the purchase price of a new General Motors car pays for the health insurance coverage of the workers who built the car.[8]

Many employers, to make up for the money they spend insuring their workers, have cut employees' salaries. Others have responded to rising insurance rates by requiring their employees to contribute more to the cost of their coverage in the form of higher co-payments, higher deductibles (the amount of medical expenses the insured must pay before insurance coverage begins), and monthly premium payments (the cost of purchasing insurance). Between 1983 and 1991, employees contributed an average of $16.47 more each month toward the cost of their employer-provided health insurance.[9]

Even workers who have comprehensive health coverage through work are not totally safe. Two-thirds of the nation's employer-provided health plans can legally be terminated at the will of the employer. The situation of John McGann, an employee in a Houston music company, demonstrates the problem.

Mr. McGann contracted AIDS. Soon after filing his first AIDs-related insurance claim, his employer reduced the lifetime limit on his AIDS-related health benefits from $1 million to $5,000. Mr. McGann's medical bills exceeded $5,000 in no time flat, and by this time Mr. McGann was too sick to be insurable elsewhere.

Mr. McGann sued his employer and lost. The judge ruled that employers must have the right to protect themselves against bankruptcy by changing the coverage they provide to their employees. The judge was concerned that fewer employers would offer their workers any health benefits at all if he interpreted the law otherwise.[10]

Employees without a clean medical record can lose their health coverage under a dangerous new practice among insurers called cherry picking. Cherry picking occurs when an insurer separates the healthy members of a group from the unhealthy members. An insurance company that covers a group of salesclerks may, for example, charge more to insure the overweight clerk with high blood pressure than the healthy twenty-five-year-old clerk who jogs three miles a day.

Cherry picking is a departure from the traditional

practice among insurers of providing every member of an insured group the same coverage for the same cost. Under these policies, sick members were not charged any more than healthy members for coverage. The extra cost of covering the unhealthy members of the group was spread out among the entire group.

The harmful effect of cherry picking is graphically demonstrated by the situation of the Renshaw family. The Renshaws had group health coverage. When their daughter Marisa was diagnosed with malfunctioning kidneys, their insurance premiums started to rise. The rates for the other members in the group stayed the same. In the course of one year, the Renshaw's rates shot up from $1,552 to $5,080. When they found themselves paying $16,000 a year for coverage, the Renshaws had to drop their insurance.[11]

The cost of private health insurance coverage has gone up steadily over the past decade. In 1980, the typical American family paid 9 percent of its annual income for health care coverage. This percentage increased to 11.7 percent in 1991. At the current rate of increase, health insurance will soon cost the average American family 16.4 percent of its annual income.[12]

In addition to the thousands of Americans who purchase insurance from private insurance companies, many elderly, poor, and disabled Americans receive their health benefits from the government. The two main government-funded health care programs are Medicare and Medicaid.

Medicare is the public health insurance program that covers the elderly and the disabled. The federal government uses tax dollars to pay the covered medical expenses of 36 million Medicare beneficiaries. Medicaid is the public medical assistance program for the poor. Under the Medicaid program, federal and state governments use tax dollars to purchase medical care for 30 million low-income individuals.[13]

Unfortunately, many elderly, disabled, and poor Americans fall through major holes in the Medicare and Medicaid nets. In 1991 Medicare only covered about 50 percent of the elderly's health care costs. This is down from 1965, when Medicare paid about 80 percent of elderly Americans' medical expenses.

Fewer poor people now qualify for Medicaid. In 1989, an Alabama family of four with an annual income of $28,750 got Medicaid; in 1992 that same family didn't qualify for medical benefits if its income exceeded $19,500.[14]

People with insurance, either private or government-funded, still suffer from the skyrocketing cost of health care because no insurance policy covers every medical expense. Few traditional fee for service plans cover costs associated with preventive care. Preventive care is medical care that helps people stay healthy. A physical examination is an example of preventive care.

Federal studies recommend a physical exam once every three years between childhood and age forty, once every two years until age sixty-five, and once a year after that.[15] Physical examinations are so important because they catch medical problems that may be brewing before the problems turn into medical crises.

Americans spend a fraction of their health care dollars on preventive care. Specifically, only 1 to 3 percent of the annual U.S. health care bill goes to preventing illness.[16] The reason so little is spent on preventive care is that most people have to pay for these medical services with their own money. They can't pass the bill along to an insurance company. Only about 35 percent of Americans with traditional types of health insurance are covered for routine physical examinations.[17]

The insurance industry defends its reluctance to cover preventive care by pointing to the historical purpose of health insurance: to protect people against financial ruin from catastrophic illness, injury, and disease. In other words, the insurance system was not developed to keep people healthy. The infrequency with which Americans get preventive care, however, drives up the cost of health care. Take, for example, the case of John, a fifty-eight-year-old steelworker. Although John felt fit as a fiddle, his wife wanted him to see a doctor. After all, John hadn't had a general checkup for over five years.

John finally gave in to his wife's urging. At the examination, John learned that he was headed for a heart attack if he didn't cut salt out of his diet and start to exercise. John followed his doctor's advice. He began snacking on carrots instead of potato chips and inviting his granddaughter over to toss a ball around. At his followup examination, John learned that his blood pressure had dropped to within normal limits.

If John had not been able to afford the $150 he paid for the physical examination, he may well have suffered a heart attack. He would have had to enter a hospital and may have required surgery. The cost of his care could easily have run into many thousands of dollars. Insurance would have paid all of these heart attack-related medical expenses.

Insurance companies, by failing to cover preventive care, save money only in the short run. Although they won't pay a couple of hundred dollars for each person they insure to get an annual physical examination, they pay hundreds of thousands of dollars to cover the costs of treating preventable medical conditions.

On an encouraging note, some insurers have started to experiment with plans that do cover preventive care. One insurer found it saved $166 each year in medical costs per person by covering preventive care.[18] Another insurer found that individuals covered for preventive care took 5.1 fewer disability days off from work.[19] The realization that short-term savings often cost more in the long run has also led at least one insurer to cover some experimental health care treatments.

Unconventional health care has traditionally been outside the scope of most insurance policies. Mutual of Omaha broke this tradition when it started covering a new heart therapy called the "reversal program." The reversal program uses a vegetarian diet and moderate exercise to control heart disease. The insurer's decision was a matter of dollars and cents. The reversal program costs one-tenth the cost of traditional heart care.[20]

Preventive and experimental care are not the only types of medical care that fall outside the scope of most insurance policies. Dental care, eye care, and prescription drugs are also rarely covered. Most insured people pay for these medical services themselves, if they can afford them.

An average American family of four has the following medical needs each year: four visits to the doctor for illness, a yearly dental checkup and follow-up dental work, prescription drugs for three members, and an eye examination and glasses for one member. These services are not covered under most insurance policies. The four visits to the doctor usually fall within the family's deductible. Dental work, prescription drugs, eye care, and preventive care are usually excluded from coverage entirely.

Even given the problems with private and government-funded insurance, such as high cost and restrictive coverage, people with insurance are a lot better off than the 38.9 million Americans who had no health insurance in 1992.[21] More than one-fourth of those uninsured are children.[22] This means that thousands of parents aren't taking children with high fevers and aching ears to the pediatrician until these symptoms blossom into full-blown medical emergencies.

Uninsured people tend to wait until their medical

problems are critical before they seek medical attention. Even then, they are more likely than insured patients to receive lower quality and less technologically advanced care. This results in the following distressing statistic: People without health insurance are more than twice as likely to die prematurely.[23]

The poor and unemployed don't make up the entire uninsured population. About 25 million of the uninsured are in families with at least one full-time wage earner.[24]

Farmworkers, construction workers, housekeepers, sales clerks, entry-level workers in fast-food restaurants, and employees of small businesses are among the nation's workers least likely to get insurance through their jobs.[25]

There are several reasons that more and more workers have no insurance coverage as a benefit of their employment. One is the most recent economic recession of 1990–91. Secure, well-paying white collar and manufacturing jobs that have always offered generous health benefits have been replaced with lower-wage temporary and part-time service jobs that often lack such benefits.

Another reason is that fewer insurers are willing to cover the employees of small businesses. Only 32 percent of companies with fewer than twenty-five employees offer their workers health insurance.[26] An insurance company that covers a group of only five employees takes a big risk. If one employee gets cancer, diabetes, heart disease, or AIDS, the insurer could end up paying out far more in medical coverage than it ever collected in premiums. Many insurers will not take the risk.

Uninsured workers often find themselves caught between a rock and a hard place. Their earnings from work disqualify them for Medicaid (the public medical assistance program for the poor), but they don't earn enough to be able to afford private insurance coverage. They are also too young to qualify for Medicare (the public insurance program for the elderly).

One of the many proposals for reforming the national health care system requires every employer to offer health coverage as an employment benefit. This proposal is commonly known as the *pay-or-play* plan. Employers who fail to play by providing their workers with coverage would have to pay money into a fund. The fund would be used to buy insurance for employees who did not receive coverage through work. The government would use tax dollars to cover the unemployed.

The clear advantage of the pay-or-play plan is universal health care coverage of every American. But the proposal also has its opponents, most notably business owners who say they can't afford to pay or play. Economists agree that many employers will suffer job losses and be forced into bankruptcy if required to pay for health coverage. There is also concern that the government would have to raise taxes to insure the unemployed.

Hawaii is the only state that currently requires employers to help buy health coverage for their employees. The system has worked well in Hawaii. Almost every Hawaiian resident has basic health insurance benefits, and Hawaiian businesses continue to thrive.

In 1988, Massachusetts also passed pay-or-play legislation. Although the reforms were supposed to go into effect in 1992, the plan was stalled by the recession. Now the reforms are supposed to go into effect by 1995, but state officials concede that a further delay or cancellation is possible.[27] Oregon and Washington State have also passed pay-or-play legislation, but opposition from the business communities in those states has delayed implementation until 1997 (Oregon) and 1999 (Washington).

With insurance companies paying most of this country's medical bills, the way insurers decide how much to pay doctors and hospitals has significant impact on the nation's health care expenses. Until recently insurance companies paid every claim, no questions asked. Insurers are now starting to ask questions.

Specifically, insurance companies are starting to ask health care providers to prove that proposed medical tests and procedures are absolutely medically necessary. The insurance companies want to make sure the doctors do not overtreat their insureds, and do not order unnecessary or excessively costly tests and procedures. This process is called *utilization review*.

When doctors call the utilization review department at Aetna Life and Casualty Insurance Company to get approval to take an MRI scan (a sophisticated type of X ray) of an insured's knee they are rejected 25 percent of the time. When they seek approval to perform a hysterectomy (the surgical removal of the uterus), the rejection rate is 10 percent.[28]

The insurance industry claims that every dollar they put into utilization review saves them up to $10 in insurance payments.[29] They realize these savings by weeding out wasteful and inappropriate medical care.

Doctors see things differently. They claim that all this second-guessing of their medical decisions by insurance companies is actually driving up the cost of health care. Take, for example, Dr. Sawyer, a surgeon. Dr. Sawyer has to pay a full-time office manager to speak with the utilization review departments of the insurance companies that insure his patients. He must also take at least an hour out of each workday to justify his patients' care to the insurers. Dr. Sawyer passes these costs along to his patients in the form of higher fees.

Utilization review is criticized on other grounds. Insurance companies, when deciding which medical services to approve and disapprove, do not rely on proven scientific standards. They tend to use arbitrary standards of review. Some insurance companies, for example, only approve hip replacements of patients who are unable to tie their shoes. There is no medical justification for this standard of review. Patients who are able to tie their shoes may need a new hip just as desperately as patients who cannot tie their shoes.

Once again, insurance companies have a different take on the situation. In their view, utilization review actually leads to *better* medical care. Patients are spared unneeded surgery and tests, doctors are stopped from ordering extra medical procedures just to fatten their own wallets, and insureds get a free second opinion when the insurance company reviews their doctors' treatment decisions.

Most private insurers, when they approve a medical service, pay the treating doctor the "reasonable and customary" charge for service. Reasonable and customary charges are the fees that most health care providers in a given geographic area charge their patients.

The way the reasonable and customary reimbursement system works is best demonstrated with an example. Say 80 percent of the doctors in Kalamazoo charge their patients $500 to treat a broken arm. Most insurance companies will pay their broken-armed policyholders in Kalamazoo up to $500 to get their arm set. Patients of the 20 percent of Kalamazoo doctors who charge more than $500 to treat a broken arm are also reimbursed only up to $500.

Reimbursement based on reasonable and customary charges encourages health care providers to maintain high fees. Doctors know that insurance companies will pay whatever most doctors in their area charge. This leads many doctors to charge their patients the same or similar high fees. Even doctors fresh out of medical school generally charge the prevailing rates for their services. Some physicians charge amounts in excess of the customary rates, figuring that their patients can afford to pay the excess amount out of pocket. In short, doctors have absolutely no incentive to lower their prices; in fact, they are under some pressure from colleagues in the local medical community to keep "reasonable and customary" charges high.

While many private insurers pay doctors based on reasonable and customary rates, they pay hospitals based on *cost-plus reimbursement*. To understand why many insurers use cost-plus reimbursement and how cost-plus payments contribute to the health care crisis, you must take a trip back in time to the birth of Blue Cross. Most hospital insurance plans are modeled after Blue Cross insurance plans.

Shortly before the Great Depression, in the late 1920s, hospitals started to feel a financial pinch. Many benefactors who had generously supported hospitals in the past had taken a bath in the stock market. Fewer and fewer patients were able to pay their bills. Hospital administrators knew they had to find a stable source of income if they were going to survive the depression.

In 1929, at Baylor University Hospital in Texas, a hospital administrator offered 1,250 schoolteachers membership in what is considered to be the forerunner of modern-day Blue Cross plans. For $6 a year, enrollees in the Baylor plan were guaranteed twenty-one days of hospital care at no additional charge. The idea behind this prepay hospital plan was to increase the flow of cash to Baylor University Hospital.

Hospitals started to band together to offer insurance plans similar to the Baylor plan. Throughout the country, groups of hospitals located close together joined forces to form nonprofit corporations. These corporations then offered local citizens prepay hospital care plans. Members of a hospital plan were entitled to care at any of the hospitals in the group. The membership fee entitled each subscriber to a semiprivate hospital room, laboratory tests, medications, and the use of an operating room at no additional cost.

These group hospital plans chose a blue cross as their symbol. The first official Blue Cross plan was established in Sacramento, California, in 1932.

Throughout the 1930s, Blue Cross organizations benefited from their close relationship with the hospital industry. The American Hospital Association (AHA) and the American Medical Association (AMA) successfully opposed efforts by the states to regulate Blue Cross in the same way other insurers were regulated. Blue Cross plans were exempted from regulations that required other insurers to set aside funds in order to handle unexpectedly large claims. Blue Cross plans were permitted to limit their payment of hospital expenses to a certain amount.

This exemption was important to Blue Cross. The driving force behind Blue Cross was to provide hospitals with a steady stream of income, not to provide members with comprehensive insurance coverage. Since catastrophic coverage was, and still is, the most expensive type of insurance, Blue Cross plans were not eager to offer this type of coverage. In return for the exemption, Blue Cross agreed to accept every applicant who sought membership in a plan.

The close ties between Blue Cross and the hospital industry were also reflected in Blue Cross's payment method. Unlike other health insurance plans of the day, Blue Cross paid hospitals directly for whatever services they provided to subscribers. Members of Blue Cross plans never received any hospital bills. With other types of insurance plans, policyholders were primarily responsible for paying their hospital bills. The insurance companies would then pay policyholders specified sums for each day that was spent in the hospital, or a specified percentage of the hospital bill. Once again, by guaranteeing payment of the bill, Blue Cross advanced the interests of the hospitals.

Blue Cross has traditionally paid hospitals on a cost-plus basis, which means that on top of being paid for the costs of providing services to their patients, hospitals also receive money from the insurance companies to cover the additional costs of building, improving, and operating their facilities. Cost-plus reimbursement is popular among hospitals because it helps them pay these maintenance and operating costs. Also, with cost-plus reimbursement, the insurers automatically pay the hospitals for just about any charge the hospitals submit. *Hospitals have had little reason to keep their costs down.*

By the 1940s, Blue Cross was the most popular hospital insurance plan. In order to compete with Blue Cross, other private insurance companies started to offer cost-plus reimbursement as well. Even today, many private insurers still reimburse on a cost-plus basis. Cost-plus reimbursement is the legacy of the old-time Blue Cross plans, which were designed by hospitals to make money for hospitals.

The cost-plus method of reimbursing hospitals has removed any incentive for hospitals to increase their efficiency. Hospitals that are run inefficiently waste money. Under the present system, many insurance companies help to pay the operating expenses of inefficiently run hospitals. As long as the hospitals can pass on to insurance companies (and the people who pay insurance premiums) the cost of their wastefulness, hospitals are not motivated to save money by increasing their efficiency.

Cost-plus reimbursement is also partially responsible for the current glut of hospitals, because the generous payments have sustained hospitals that would otherwise have gone out of business. On average, hospitals in the United States are filled only to 64.5 percent of capacity.[30] Every night nearly 40 percent of all hospital beds are empty.[31] This means that American hospitals are losing between $6 billion and $8 billion a year in overhead costs that are not reimbursed by insurance.[32]

The oversupply of hospitals has caused intense competition in the hospital industry. Hospitals compete against each other for referrals of patients from doctors. Some hospitals "buy" patient referrals by paying doctors honorariums and hiring them as board members. Other hospitals put large amounts of money into advertising budgets. All of these expenses are passed on to hospitalized patients in the form of higher bills.

Excessive numbers of hospitals also mean that each hospitalized patient pays a greater share of the costs of running the hospital. When a hospital is filled to capacity, more patients share the financial burden of the operating expenses. Hospitals with many empty beds must charge each paying patient more.

Today Blue Cross and Blue Shield is an organization of seventy-one independent nonprofit insurance companies. These companies provide health insurance to 68 million Americans in all fifty states. Twenty of the seventy-one Blue Cross plans offer insurance to any applicant who can pay for it, regardless of health; the rest of the plans reject applicants with serious health problems.

Recently Empire Blue Cross and Blue Shield, the Blue Cross plan that services New York, came under fire for losing tens of millions of dollars. Executives of the plan were found to have earned unreasonably high salaries ($600,000 a year for the chairman) and benefited from excessively high corporate living (first-class travel and chauffeur-driven Lincoln Town Cars); poor customer service was found to have driven away many major corporate customers; and millions of dollars were found to have been wasted on politically connected consultants and lobbyists.[33]

A number of proposals have been made to reform the insurance system, ranging from requiring insurers to charge uniform rates to all consumers to prohibiting insurers from canceling the policies of people who get sick.

The insurance industry complains that such requirements would force them out of business. Large insurance companies favor reform plans that are based on a system of managed competition. Managed competition plays an important role for large insurers. (See chapter 9.)

The insurance industry has every intention of flexing its awesome political muscle to push through reform plans that promote its own best interests. The industry has the ability to influence Congress through generous campaign contributions. In the first half of 1993 alone, insurance companies gave $1.7 million in congressional contributions.[34]

The insurance industry also commits millions of dollars to advertising campaigns designed to win the public's support. For example, the Coalition of Health Insurance Choices, a group of insurers, announced a $4 million television and newspaper campaign to convince consumers of the need to fight for the right to choose their own insurance carrier.[35] The insurance industry's advertising blitz only promises to become more intense as health care reform comes closer to becoming a reality.

Of course, the salaries of insurance lobbyists and advertising executives are all passed along to the insurance consumer in the form of inflated premiums. And so it goes.

THE HIGH PRICE OF HIGH TECHNOLOGY

HAS MEDICAL RESEARCH GONE COMPLETELY OUT OF CONTROL?

*S*cientists can be proud of a number of extraordinary technological achievements in the field of medicine. Many major organs can now be transplanted. Mechanical devices are available to replace failing joints, hearts, lungs, and kidneys. Machines capable of sustaining life can take over when all vital signs have stopped. Artificial blood, veins, and skin can all be manufactured in the laboratory.

The origins of today's technological explosion date back to the early 1800s, when the stethoscope was first invented. Other historic landmarks in the evolution of medical technology include the discovery of anesthesia in the 1840s, the discovery of sterile surgical procedures in the 1870s, and the discovery of X-ray technology in the late 1800s.

In the 1930s and 1940s, during the pharmaceutical revolution, doctors became able to control infectious diseases for the first time through the discovery of antibiotics and vaccines. By the 1950s, they could keep patients alive with the heart-lung machine.

Ninety percent of the medicine being practiced today did not exist in 1950. Doctors now have more tools at their disposal with which to detect and cure illnesses, but this technological boom has not come without costs. *Medicine's increased reliance on high technology has significantly contributed to the upward spiral of health care costs.*

New technologies tend to be overused. Magnetic resonance imaging (MRI) scanners, for example, were invented to treat patients who had serious head injuries. But medical equipment manufacturers produced lots and lots of MRI machines. Before long, MRI machines found their way into many hospitals, medical centers, and doctors' offices across the country. Doctors began administering MRI scans to patients who complained of headaches, dizziness, and other vague symptoms. Such frequent use, possibly overuse, of CAT (computerized axial tomography) scanners, at a cost of $1,000 a scan, has imposed enormous expense on the health care system.

A look at the numbers reveals the enormity of the expense. MRI scans detect life-threatening conditions in one out of two patients with head trauma. This means that for every $2,000 of health care dollars spent (two scans for two patients at $1,000 a scan), one patient's life is saved. When prescribed for patients complaining of headaches and dizziness (not head traumas), the chance of finding a treatable condition drops to one in 2,000. This means that for every $2 million spent (2,000 scans for 2,000 patients at $1,000 a scan), one life is saved.[1] Although it's impossible to put a price tag on human life, this country may not be able to afford to spend $2 million to save one life when millions of Americans lack even basic health care.

Laparoscopic surgery is another example of an overused high-tech medical procedure. Laparoscopic surgery was invented as an alternative to standard gallbladder surgery. The procedure offered patients the benefits of less pain, shorter hospital stays, and quicker recoveries.

Now doctors are starting to use laparoscopic

surgery for appendectomies (the removal of the appendix). An appendectomy is already a relatively simple operation. Patients experience little pain and recover quickly. Laparoscopic appendectomies neither reduce postoperative pain nor shorten hospital stays. But a laparoscopic appendectomy costs more than a traditional appendectomy because laparoscopic surgery requires the use of costly specialized instruments.[2]

Ultrasound (the use of sound waves to produce an image of a fetus) is a final example of an overused medical technology. Most doctors advise pregnant patients to undergo two ultrasound scans during their pregnancy at a cost of $200 a scan. With about 4 million American women getting pregnant each year, the amount of money spent on ultrasound scans each year pushes $1 billion.[3] The routine use of ultrasound technology is unnecessary in 80 percent of all pregnancies. In these low-risk pregnancies, there are no medical benefits from the test (although they may provide protection against malpractice suits).[4]

In addition to driving up costs through overuse, advances in medical technology and knowledge may also encourage medical specialization, which in turn drives up health care spending. Specialists undergo extra training to become experts in particular medical procedures and illnesses. They charge higher fees and perform more costly tests and services.

The increased number of medical specialists has also meant a decline in the number of physicians in general practice. Some experts believe that medical students may not feel capable of mastering the mind-boggling amount of information that is required today to treat a wide variety of medical conditions. In 1992, the percentage of medical students entering the field of general internal medicine was less than 15 percent.[5] In the 1920s, when more than half of all medical school graduates went into general practice, most body systems and diseases were still largely a mystery.

Technology-related forces also lead to waste in the hospital industry. Due to the oversupply of hospitals, hospitals have to compete against each other for referrals of patients from doctors. To impress doctors and attract patient referrals, every hospital purchases the very latest in medical technology. The result has been costly inefficiency. Too many hospitals are equipped with the same expensive state-of-the-art medical equipment. And, until recently, public and private payers rewarded such capital expansion.

The prevalence of magnetic resonance imaging (MRI) scanners demonstrates the problem. Within a two-mile radius of New York's North Shore University Hospital, there are at least three hospital-based scanners and seven more scanners in private medical centers. Patients pay for all of these scanners when they pay their medical bills. At a cost of about $1.5 million a scanner, American health care consumers have spent a tidy sum on these machines.[6]

Investing in medical equipment is all the rage among health care providers. A quick look at the numbers shows why. A single MRI scan costs about $1,000. A scanner costs about $1.5 million. Any doctor, hospital, or medical center that buys a scanner has to perform only 2,500 scans a year (that's just over 200 a month) to make an easy million-dollar annual profit on its investment.

These figures may explain why there are 2,000 MRI scanners in the United States, and only 25 in all of England. Medicine is a private profit-making industry in this country. In England, it's not. The government provides the British with their health care. Providers in England don't stand to make money off costly medical tests.

The MRI epidemic only promises to get worse. A

recent study found that MRI scanners will soon be more accurate than mammography for detecting breast cancer. Each year about 30 million women have mammograms. Most pay about $75 each for the test. If MRIs become the accepted method of screening for breast cancer, the cost of the test will increase to $1,000. The total cost to the health care system will reach billions of dollars. But this cost may be justified by the anticipated 100 percent accuracy rate of the MRI scans in detecting breast tumors, compared to the 33 percent error rate of mammography.[7]

The cost of an MRI scan may go even higher thanks to research into the dye used by most MRI scanners. The dye, while inexpensive and basically safe, causes about 300 deaths a year. Scientists recently discovered an alternative dye that is 100 percent safe. The cost of the new dye is about $1 billion a year.[8] Again, the question arises whether the additional degree of safety (300 lives a year) is worth the added expense.

Doctors, with the help of scientists and medical researchers, are getting better and better at keeping people alive. Patients can now survive many serious illnesses that used to be fatal. Infectious diseases, for example, were a major cause of childhood deaths. Now, with the widespread availability of antibiotics, people are living longer and dying of diseases that are more costly to treat, such as cancer.

AIDS presents a graphic example of an illness that used to be terminal until scientists discovered AZT. AZT doesn't cure AIDs, but it extends the lives of many AIDS patients. There is no question that AZT is a godsend to AIDS sufferers and society alike. However, the economic implications of AZT cannot be ignored. In addition to the expense of the medication itself, AZT patients require costly monitoring and treatment for infections and anemia. Once again, there is a trade-off: Can Americans continue to pay such enormous sums?

Doctors no longer view death as inevitable. They confront death like an enemy, to be fought back with all of the high-tech tools at their disposal. Doctors have become so skillful at prolonging life that many view a patient's death as a personal failure. Death is no longer accepted as the natural end to life.

Doctors are trained to treat dying patients aggressively with open heart massage and massive doses of antibiotics, for example. These "heroic" measures are not always in the patient's best interest. Sometimes the benefits of a few more months of life are outweighed by the patient's added pain and suffering. Given the choice, many patients would prefer a peaceful and dignified death.

Doctors can now revive a patient in cardiac arrest, whose heart has stopped beating. The cost of reviving such a patient exceeds $150,000. Unfortunately, despite this huge expenditure of money, few revived patients ever regain the ability to breathe on their own. Most spend their final days in the intensive care unit of a hospital, hooked up to expensive life-support systems. Nevertheless, the policy in almost every hospital is to attempt revival of every cardiac arrest patient who has not expressed a wish not to be revived.[9]

Scientists are intrigued by the challenge of keeping patients alive, even when there is no heartbeat or pulse. On any given day, between 5,000 and 10,000 people in a persistent vegetative state (permanent coma) are being kept alive at a cost of about $75,000 a year each.[10]

Doctors themselves are uncomfortable using such advanced technology to keep dying patients alive. Most doctors and nurses think too much is done to keep terminally ill patients alive. Seventy percent of resident physicians interviewed reported acting against their consciences in overtreating patients for whom death was imminent and who had no chance of recovery.[11] More than half of providers polled indicated that respirators, cardiopulmonary resuscitation, tube feedings, and kidney dialysis are overused in the treatment of dying patients. To avoid such extraordinary efforts, patients must make "living wills" or give advance directions to their physcians.[12]

Some doctors have been accused of causing dying patients to continue suffering so the doctor can try out a new technology. Such experimentation is sometimes justified on the ground that there is a chance, however slim, that use of the new technology will extend the patient's life. Or the experimentation is defended as an attempt to learn something that will help keep other patients alive. Medical experimentation done without the patient's informed consent is always wrong.

People who survive serious illnesses with the help of medical technology are often left disabled, unable to walk, feed, bathe, or groom themselves. Older adults, who now live longer than ever,[13] can survive with these types of chronic disabilities for thirty years or more. About 7 million disabled Americans need help with their daily activities at home or in a nursing home. This number is expected to double by the year 2030.[14]

The cost of providing such extensive care on a long-term basis can be astronomical. In 1990, the nation spent $42 billion on nursing home care and $8 billion caring for chronically ill patients at home. By the year 2020, long-term care will consume $500 billion health care dollars a year if current rates of spending continue.[15] However, it is also true that high-tech medicine has enabled many people to live many more productive years.

The ability to prolong life has even changed the way doctors view themselves. Before physicians became so good at saving lives with advanced medical technology they saw themselves primarily as comforters. Doctors practicing medicine at the turn of the century could not cure many illnesses, so they focused their efforts on making their patients as comfortable as possible. They treated their patients' symptoms and eased their patients' anxiety.

Advances in medical technology have raised the public's expectations about what medicine can accomplish. Many Americans now believe that every ailment can be cured if enough research dollars are thrown at the problem. This perception has shifted attention away from low-tech, inexpensive ways Americans can extend their lifespan.

The benefits of a healthy lifestyle cannot be overstated. Poor health habits have been linked to early death and chronic disabilities. Overeating, physical inactivity, smoking, drinking too much alcohol, sleeping too little or too much, eating between meals, and skipping breakfast have all been found to contribute to premature death and disability. People who practice six or seven of these poor health habits are twice as likely to become disabled as those with no more than two of these habits.[16] Eight of the ten leading causes of death are related to lifestyle, including eating, exercise, and smoking habits.[17]

People do not seem to take these findings seriously. Sixty-six percent of Americans are overweight, only 33 percent exercise vigorously three or more times a week, and only 50 percent get seven to eight hours of sleep a night.[18]

Perhaps the most disturbing statistic of all is that 24 percent of adult Americans still smoke cigarettes, one of the most costly habits of all.[19] Cigarette smoking and other forms of tobacco use add $22 billion to annual health care costs.[20]

Other types of life-shortening social behavior also

increase America's health care bill. Nearly 25 percent of the $666 billion Americans spend on health care goes to treat victims of drug abuse, domestic violence (such as wife abuse), crime, and other harmful social behavior. Failure to use seat belts and smoke detectors, dangerous recreational activities, and unprotected sex also contribute to escalating health care costs.[21]

Alcohol abuse is responsible for another $85 billion of annual health care dollars.[22] Older Americans are hospitalized more for alcohol-related problems than heart attacks. The treatment of these alcohol-related conditions costs the taxpayer over $230 million a year in Medicare payments.[23] More reliance on a healthy lifestyle would decrease the use of costly technology and have better results.

The high cost of treating people at the end of their lives is matched by the cost of treating premature babies who are at the very beginning of their lives. Thanks to major advances in neonatal (newborn) medical technology, doctors can now keep alive babies who weigh only one pound at birth.

Take, for example, Alexandra. Alexandra was born three and a half months early, weighing less than 20 ounces. The cost of saving Alexandra's life topped a quarter of a million dollars.[24] As Alexandra grew, her medical bills grew with her. At two years of age, she was being seen by specialists in pediatrics, neurology, heart, asthma, hearing, and eyes at least twenty-four times a year. Her medicine each week to prevent seizures and to help her breathe cost $150 each week. She was also attending special-education classes at a cost of $375 a week.[25]

The medical costs of caring for a premature baby often continue after birth. Extremely premature babies are at heightened risk of developing serious mental and physical disabilities. They have a one-in-five chance of developing cerebral palsy, mental retardation, seizure disorders, respiratory problems, blindness, and deafness. Three out of four never catch up with their peers in school.[26]

All of the research dollars being spent developing even more fantastic ways to prolong life might be redirected if the public had a greater say over the funding of medical research. Unfortunately, the public has remarkably little control over the direction of scientific exploration, despite the government's substantial role in paying the salaries of medical researchers.

Medical research is virtually unregulated by government. Well-funded organizations of drug and medical equipment manufacturers have successfully lobbied public officials to oppose government regulation of medical research.[27] The scientific community's insulation from the public has led valuable resources to be devoted to the development of technologies that interest scientists but do not necessarily benefit large numbers of people.

There is no question that the very old and the very sick consume more than their share of the nation's health care dollars. In fact, 30 percent of America's health care budget goes to treat only 1 percent of the population.[28] Can society afford the heroic measures necessary to keep death away from these patients, or should the money be spent providing relatively low-cost medical services to larger numbers of Americans?

This question raises the delicate issue of health care rationing. Rationing medical care means denying needed health services to certain people because medical resources are limited. The concept of rationing medical care is foreign to most Americans. In this country, every citizen is believed to have an equal right to the best medical care available. No one should be denied an organ transplant, for example, because the procedure costs too much or because the patient is too poor.

Oregon is the only state that has dared to face head-on the question of rationing health care. The state recently overhauled its Medicaid program (medical assistance to the poor) so that it now rations medical services for low-income residents. Medicaid beneficiaries in Oregon are no longer covered for every high-cost, high-risk, low-benefit medical procedure they want.

Oregon Medicaid officials ranked 688 medical procedures according to how much the procedures cost and how much they benefited patients, and denied Medicaid coverage for procedures ranked 565 through 688 (a total of 119 procedures). For example, Medicaid beneficiaries in Oregon who have cancer are not covered for liver transplants, and no Medicaid beneficiaries are covered for treatments related to the common cold and backache.[29]

Oregon made these changes in its Medicaid program so that it could ease eligibility requirements. It is now easier to get Medicaid in Oregon than in most other states in the country. With these reforms, 120,000 more poor people in Oregon qualify for Medicaid coverage of their basic health care expenses.[30]

The New York Medicaid program also rations health care, in a way. In New York, Medicaid beneficiaries are covered for only ten doctor visits, eighteen laboratory tests, three dental visits, and forty-three drugstore purchases.

These restrictions can lead to tragedy, as in the case of Glenda Maldonado, an unemployed mother of three and a Medicaid recipient. Glenda only had three Medicaid-covered doctor visits left when her young son developed a high fever. Instead of taking her child right to the doctor, and risking wasting one of her remaining visits, she decided to wait until the morning. By that time, her son was dead of bacterial meningitis.[31]

Before you blame the New York Medicaid program

for the death of Glenda Maldonado's son, it is important to consider the alternatives. New York could have covered every Medicaid recipient for more doctors' visits, more lab tests, and more drugstore purchases, but this would have left fewer Medicaid dollars to go around. The Medicaid program would have had to tighten its eligibility requirements, leaving more poor people without any medical benefits at all. New York Medicaid officials determined that limiting the number of Medicaid-covered services was the lesser of two evils.

The country was recently faced with the conflict between limited health care resources and the ethics of fighting for life in the case of Angela and Amy Lakeberg. Angela and Amy were Siamese twins who shared a single heart. Doctors said they could surgically separate the twins, but one baby would definitely die and the other baby had only a slim chance of survival. The parents decided to go ahead with the surgery. Angela survived. Amy died.

The cost to the medical system of separating Angela and Amy Lakeberg reached hundreds of thousands of dollars. Each day the babies were in the intensive care unit of the hospital cost $1,800.[32] Would the money spent trying to save the life of one very ill Siamese twin have been better spent providing basic medical care to hundreds of uninsured Americans? Or would depriving the Lakebergs of even the *small* chance of saving one daughter's life have violated America's most fundamental values? Tough questions.

Despite the difficult issues raised by America's technological achievements, the pace of medical research is unlikely to slow down anytime soon. Private industry is now deeply involved in the business of medical research. Scientists in laboratories across the country have financial agreements with private health care corporations. These corporations have a financial interest in the products under development and promise to share their earnings from profitable discoveries with the researchers.

Private industry's financial involvement in medical research has introduced economic considerations in the selection of research priorities. Corporations that manufacture and sell medical machinery pay scientists well to research technologies that will require expensive medical equipment, while scientists who are searching for a cure to, say, parasitic diseases are left scrounging for research dollars. Why? Because parasitic diseases mostly affect residents of poor rural areas and inner-city ghettos. Curing these diseases doesn't promise to make a profit for multinational corporations.

Research projects that attract the most money are not always the ones that provide the largest numbers of people with the greatest health benefits. Research into ways medical care can be provided more efficiently and cheaply, for example, would serve the health care needs of huge numbers of Americans. But private companies that profit from the existing costly and inefficient health care system are unlikely to pay scientists to solve what they view as a nonproblem.

Private industry's involvement in medical research also raises some ethical concerns. Are corporations trustworthy enough to resist the lure of large profits in order to protect the public interest? The answer to this question was no in the case of DES. Researchers developed the drug DES when they discovered a way to manufacture the female hormone estrogen in the laboratory. Private manufacturers of DES promoted the drug as a miracle pill to prevent miscarriages.

The manufacturers continued making this claim despite ten years of evidence that DES was ineffective. Scientists later found a high rate of cancer, infertility, and other problems in daughters of women who had taken DES during pregnancy. The effectiveness and safety of DES might have been more thoroughly researched if the private corporations that paid for the scientific research had not been so eager to profit from their investment.

Perhaps the question of where the nation should put its research dollars is raised most pointedly by our experience with the artificial heart. To date, the federal government has invested over $200 million developing a mechanical heart to take the place of a failing human heart. Despite this substantial commitment of resources, scientists have still not produced a satisfactory artificial heart.

In 1985 an artificial heart was used for the first time as a temporary bridge to a heart transplant. The patient was on the Jarvik-7 artificial heart for nine days before receiving a human heart. Five years later, the Jarvik-7 was banned except for emergency use when the Food and Drug Administration (FDA) found defects in a number of its mechanical parts. In 1991 the Jarvik-7 was banned altogether after its manufacturer went out of business.

The artificial heart being used today is almost identical to the Jarvik-7. It can still be used only to keep patients alive temporarily until a human heart can be found, and it is still powered by a unit the size of a large television set. The longest-surviving recipient of an experimental portable, battery-powered heart pump died after sixteen months. In January 1993 the artificial heart was used for the first time in nearly two years.[33]

There are at least two hundred different ways the $200 million that has been invested in the still-unsuccessful artificial heart could have been used to provide greater health benefits to more people. But helping the most people is not the only goal of medical research. And maybe it shouldn't be.

America leads the world in medical research.

Thanks to the efforts of American scientists, doctors worldwide have a more complete understanding of the human body than was ever thought possible.

Also, not every advanced medical technology suffers defects such as the artificial heart has. Technological advances in medication have conquered previously fatal or disabling diseases, such as scarlet fever, cholera, yellow fever, typhoid, leprosy, malaria, scurvy, rubella, measles, and whooping cough. Controlling these serious medical conditions has cut down on human suffering and has saved the health care system money that would otherwise have been spent treating victims of these diseases.

Unfortunately, though, medical technology is not always a cure. Technological advances have also *caused* new diseases and illnesses. In the field of pharmaceutical research, for example, the cost of medicine's extraordinary technological achievements in terms of public health is particularly clear. Each year, a million people are hospitalized for treatment of bad side effects to newly developed prescription drugs; about 130,000 of these people die every year.

There are a number of reasons for these frightening statistics. The Food and Drug Administration (FDA) does not have the budget or the manpower to regulate adequately the huge volume of drugs that enter the market. Often it is not even possible to discover every possible harmful effect of a drug before the drug hits the market. Furthermore, even when the FDA does approve a drug for a particular use, physicians frequently prescribe the drug for purposes never considered by the FDA. Finally, many drugs, such as tranquilizers, are overused. This often leads to harmful, or even fatal, addictions.

The FDA's track record for testing the safety of medical equipment is also far from perfect. A 1993 FDA review of the agency's own safety studies showed that some tests were so poorly carried out that they were "not up to the level of fifth-grade science."[34] Some devices found to have been poorly tested included a heart defibrillator (used to regulate heartbeats) and a laser device used to unclog blood vessels.

The FDA undertook the review after some widely used and approved medical devices failed. A defective heart valve was taken off the market in 1985, and harmful silicone-gel breast implants in 1992. In an effort to explain the lapses in safety testing, the FDA points to a loss of employees, an increase in the number and complexity of applications, and a commitment of their limited resources to AIDS drugs and other life-saving remedies.[35]

Health risks are not the only threat posed by medical technology. Advanced medical machinery may also alter the traditional doctor-patient relationship. Today doctors understand diseases on a cellular and molecular level. In many cases, they have no reason to talk to their patients at all. They can get all the information they need by using sophisticated technologies that study the inside and outside of their patients' bodies. As a result, doctors may neglect the emotional needs of their patients, leaving the patient feeling like nothing more than a body carrying an illness— not a person.

Medicine used to be much more "hands on." Doctors would run their palms over their patients' bodies to detect tumorous lumps. They would move their patients' limbs to diagnose sprains and fractures. They would tap their patients' chests to pick up heartbeat irregularities. These practices are changing. Highly sophisticated diagnostic imaging machines are now used to find tumors. X rays locate breaks and tears, and electrocardiograms monitor heartbeats.

Probably the most dramatic example of medical technology's potential to disrupt the doctor-patient relationship is telemedicine. With telemedicine, doctors use the telephone and television to treat patients located miles away. Telemedicine may well redefine health care over the next decade.

Telemedicine has been used to send pictures of rashes to faraway dermatologists (skin specialists), and pictures of jugular veins to distant cardiologists (heart specialists). Telemedicine was used to teach a six-year-old stroke victim in the small town of Cuba, New York, how to walk again. Rehabilitation specialists 85 miles away in Buffalo, the closest big city, used videos to teach the girl exercises and to monitor her progress.

The future of telemedicine is almost unlimited. Telemedicine can enable doctors to treat prison inmates without ever moving the inmates to an emergency room. Ambulance paramedics stuck in traffic will be able to use telemedicine to provide emergency assistance to the patients they transport. Doctors at remote rural clinics will be able to use telemedicine to send X rays of injured residents to radiologists in city hospitals. Patients will be able to recover from surgery at home, with hospital doctors monitoring their heart rate, blood pressure, and temperature over the phone. Doctors in Texas will be able to help treat patients in Russia, Turkey, and Saudi Arabia.

Critics warn that telemedicine will drive up health care costs yet again. The price of the cameras and other equipment used in telemedicine is upwards of $50,000, and the cost of a transmitting station can top $1 million. And with medical specialists just a phone call away, the use of high-priced experts will likely increase.

Finally, opponents of telemedicine are concerned about patient privacy. Information that passes electronically can always be intercepted.

Supporters of telemedicine dispute that this new

technology will increase health care costs. They argue that costs will come down. With doctors and specialists so readily available, hospitals and medical centers across the country will be able to hire more lower-paid nurses and physician assistants. These savings, in theory, can be passed along to patients and insurers.[36]

There is no question that America's development of innovative medical technology is impressive. But does every American have access to technological advances? Apparently not, for, according to studies, 37 million uninsured Americans receive only 50 to 70 percent of the medical care that fully insured patients receive. The uninsured are also about half as likely as the well-insured to enter a hospital, and about 25 percent as likely to see a physician.[37] Black Americans wait twice as long for kidney transplants as white Americans.[38]

Low-income individuals covered under Medicaid, the medical assistance program for the poor, also have limited access to the latest in medical care. There is a shortage of doctors and medical centers that accept Medicaid's low payment rate. Even middle-class individuals with private insurance often have to forgo costly new medical tests and services because they cannot afford the deductible and co-payments.

The equity of access to medical care in this country has not improved over the past ten years. Almost half as many black women receive prenatal care as white. Fewer than half of women with incomes under $25,000 have had a least one mammogram test for breast cancer screening.[39] Black Americans, while more likely to suffer heart attacks than whites, are far less likely to have bypass surgery, an angiogram (insertion of dye into the coronary artery for heart X ray), and angioplasty (insertion of balloon to expand a clogged artery).[40]

Hopefully, if health care reform is successful, medical technology will be available to treat every American, not just the rich and well-insured. But more health care will mean more health care spending—anywhere from $33 billion to $50 billion more in 1994, according to government estimates.[41] This is a hefty price tag; is universal access to the most advanced medical care worth it? Another tough question to ponder as you move on to the next chapter.

THE BIG BUSINESS
OF MEDICINE

HAS HEALTH CARE IN AMERICA BECOME JUST ANOTHER INDUSTRY?

ealth care in the United States has become big business—so big, in fact, that the health care industry is expected to consume $940 billion in 1993, employ 10.6 million people, export $16 billion worth of medical and pharmaceutical supplies, and operate 6,600 hospitals.[1] Hospital services in 1991 cost $288.6 billion or 38 percent of total health care costs. The defense industry, America's second largest industry after health care, will likely consume only $290 billion, employ only 5.4 million people, export only $10 billion of equipment, and operate only 50 military bases in 1993.[2]

A lot of people make their living in health care. Between 1988 and 1992, while private employment rose only about 1 percent, total employment in the health care industry rose 43 percent.[3] Doctors, nurses, orderlies, linen suppliers, and food manufacturers are some of the obvious workers in the cast of health care employees. Less obvious are the executives and shareholders of corporations that invest heavily in the health care industry.

Corporate investment in health care is still a fairly recent development. Until about forty years ago, few hospitals were in business to make money for outside investors. Most hospitals were either publicly owned (by state or local governments) or not for profit (owned by private or nonprofit organizations with the earnings reinvested in the hospital to cover operating expenses). The first for-profit hospital that made money for outside investors was established in the late 1950s.

Corporate-owned, for-profit hospitals are the clearest example of a general trend toward the industrialization of medicine. A growing number of American hospitals are being run like any other business—to make money for the corporations that own them. Corporate executives, with their expertise in finance and real estate, are managing facilities that used to be run by staff physicians with an expertise in medicine.

What does this trend mean for health care in America? Does it mean that the focus will shift away from patient care and onto the bottom line of the health care corporation's annual report?

The idea of allowing investors to make a profit from hospitals was thought up by Dr. Thomas Frist, Sr., a cardiologist. Dr. Frist sold shares in Park View Hospital to outside investors to raise money to expand the hospital. In exchange for a sum of money, the investors became entitled to share in the hospital's future earnings.

When the Medicare and Medicaid programs were established,investors saw an opportunity to make a healthy profit from the major influx of public money into the health care system. Through Medicare, the government began paying many of the medical expenses of the elderly and the disabled. Through Medicaid, the government began buying health care for the poor. At this time, outside investors started to pump more and more money into private hospitals.

With investments in nonprofit hospitals up, hospital chains were soon born. Again, Dr. Frist was at the forefront of this development, realizing that he could reduce his costs and increase his efficiency by combining ownership of a number of hospitals. Dr. Frist named his chain of hospitals the Hospital Corporation of America (HCA). Within six months, HCA controlled eleven hospitals. After fifteen years, HCA was running almost four hundred hospitals and paying its chief executive officer the second highest executive salary in the country.

Oil and chemical companies, such as Dow Chemical, Monsanto, and Standard Oil, started to get into health care investing in the late 1970s. These companies bought shares in existing health care corporations and set up their own health care businesses. These corporate giants brought more private money into the health care industry, and health care companies became less subject to public regulation. Nevertheless, in 1991 the government paid 56.4 percent of the cost of hospital services.

Throughout the 1980s, for-profit hospital chains continued to experience tremendous growth. By 1983, the fastest-growing sector of American industry was for-profit hospital corporations. Within a couple of years, the number of for-profit hospital chains increased by 20 percent. Stocks for the top four hospital chains rose by 30 percent, and the profits of the twenty largest chains shot up almost 40 percent (a phenomenal rate of profit). By the mid-1980s, about 12 percent of all acute-care hospitals (hospitals that provide short-term intensive medical treatment) were for-profit facilities.

In 1990 there were seventy-two for-profit hospital chains, four of which dominated the field: Hospital Corporation of America, American Medical International, Humana, and National Medical Enterprises. The combined earnings of these four chains topped

$15.5 billion. By 1991, almost 25 percent of all private acute-care hospitals were owned by corporate investors.

A June 1993 merger of Galen Health Care, Inc., and the Columbia Hospital Corporation demonstrates the magnitude of America's health care giants. The merger, valued at about $4.1 billion, created the largest U.S. hospital chain, with 99 hospitals (over 22,000 beds) and revenues projected to exceed $5 billion in 1993.[4]

Corporate-owned, profit-making hospitals are not the only example of the industrialization of medicine in America. Another developing trend is the corporate purchase of medical practices. Doctors are selling their practices to corporations in increasing numbers. Take, for example, the sale of several group practices in Oklahoma City and Houston to Caremark International, a health care corporation with annual revenues of $1.9 billion. Caremark paid the doctors cash and stock to buy their practices. The company also entered into employment contracts with the doctors. The doctors agreed to work for Caremark for a period of years for a salary, and Caremark agreed to purchase new buildings, medical equipment, and computers for the doctors, pay the doctors' malpractice insurance premiums, hire nurses and receptionists, and manage the medical practices.[5]

The lure of financial security attracts many doctors to corporate purchasers. Doctors employed by a corporation are guaranteed a steady income. They do not have to worry about price controls and other reform proposals that threaten to reduce their income. Although they sacrifice some independence by becoming corporate employees, many feel they will lose this independence anyway under health care reform.

Corporations buy hospitals and medical practices for one reason and one reason only: to make money for their investors. Health care is so attractive to corporate investors because the health care industry has traditionally had almost total freedom to set its own prices.

Compare the health care industry with the oil industry. Oil companies have to compete against one another. When there is a glut of oil on the market, prices come down. Each oil company must fight for the business of oil consumers by lowering the cost of their product.

In the health care industry, however, doctors, hospitals, drug manufacturers, and nursing homes determine what their own goods and services are worth. They are in this unique position because few health care consumers pay their own bills. Insurance companies pay most of their bills for them. (See chapter 2.) People aren't as motivated to shop around for a well-priced hospital as they are to find the gas station with the lowest price per gallon.

Health care is also attractive to investors because it is practically recession proof. With most other products, when money gets tight, people can cut back on consumption. But when people need hospital care, they need hospital care—regardless of their financial situation (although the poor and the uninsured do forgo basic health care).

Critics of the industrialization of health care raise a number of interesting concerns: Is it right for investors to profit from the illness of others? Or should medical care be a fundamental human right that is equally available to all, without regard to economic considerations?

The United States is the only industrialized country other than South Africa in which investors profit from health care. In Canada, England, Germany, and Sweden, the government pays the nation's medical bills. Health care is provided to every citizen, rich and poor alike.

The growth of for-profit hospitals has led to several changes in the U.S. hospital industry, some good and some bad. One of the most positive developments has been increased hospital efficiency. Many for-profit health care corporations have reduced their operating expenses by making bulk purchases of supplies and equipment, sharing high-priced technological equipment, using management specialists, and imposing corporate discipline. (These savings have not been passed on to consumers, however.)

A less fortunate consequence of corporate hospital ownership has been a reduction in the availability of hospital care for the poor. For-profit hospitals are less likely to treat patients who can't afford to pay for their care. Nowhere is this problem more evident than in the increased incidence of "patient dumping."

Patient dumping occurs when for-profit private hospitals transfer nonpaying patients to public hospitals—government-owned facilities that treat low-income and uninsured patients.

Many public hospitals are on the brink of bankruptcy. They simply don't receive enough funds from federal, state, and local governments to finance the treatment of the thousands of patients who come through their doors. Cutbacks in the Medicaid program haven't helped. More than 1 million people lost their Medicaid benefits between 1981 and 1985. New York's public hospitals lost $152 million in 1990 and $230 million in 1991.

Desperate financial times have forced public hospitals to tighten their belts. They have had to reduce the number of available beds, cut staff, postpone building repairs, and keep outdated medical equipment. All of these cost-cutting measures are being taken at a time when the demand for the services of public hospitals is increasing.

Financially troubled public hospitals are attractive takeover targets of the for-profit hospital corporations.

Between 1981 and 1986, 180 public hospitals were taken over by profit-making companies and turned into for-profit hospitals. A number of small, nonprofit community hospitals have also been bought by wealthy corporations.

The new corporate owners of the public facilities use money they raise by selling stock to investors to fix up the dilapidated buildings and purchase the latest technological equipment. The revamped for-profit hospitals are then able to attract referrals of well-insured patients from private physicians.

So where does this leave the poor patients who used to go to these public and community hospitals? Sitting in the even more crowded emergency rooms of the fewer remaining public and nonprofit facilities, that's where.

A related problem with for-profit hospital chains is high prices. For-profit facilities set their fees as high as the market will bear. Many maximize their earnings by offering highly specialized medical services, the convenience of costly on-site pharmacy and laboratory services, and such fringe benefits as valet parking.

Many private hospitals also boost their earnings by advertising their services. In an effort to attract private, paying patients, these hospitals publicize the benefits of elective surgery by showing before-and-after pictures of tummy tucks and face-lifts. And to attract well-insured pregnant women they may show off birthing rooms that provide all the comforts of home. These advertising costs are passed along to the patients of the hospital in higher fees.

The inflated prices charged by for-profit hospitals are well demonstrated by two studies that were conducted in the early 1980s. One study showed charges at for-profit hospitals to be 24 percent higher than the rates at nonprofit hospitals and 47 percent higher than public hospitals. The second study showed that for-profit hospitals charged their patients between 6 and 58 percent more than nonprofit hospitals for the delivery of babies, the removal of gallbladders, and hysterectomies.[6]

To increase their earnings, some health care corporations have even taken doctors' offices to the mall and invested in storefront clinic franchises. These corporate-owned medical clinics treat patients on a walk-in basis in malls across the country. Clinics with names like MedFirst and EmergiCare are staffed by doctors who charge relatively low hourly rates. The clinics are usually open normal business hours, say 9:00 A.M. to 5:00 P.M., and see patients without appointment.

Although the clinics make money for their corporate owners, it is not clear that people who go to the clinics receive quality care. For one thing, the doctors that staff the clinics have no ongoing relationship with their patients. They have only minimal knowledge of the patient's past medical history and do not followup with patients after the clinic visit. Patients just pass through the clinic doors, leaving the doctors minimally accountable for the medical care they provide.

Finally, health care corporations increase their earnings by pressuring doctors who work in their facilities to maximize corporate profits. Corporate executives may, for example, encourage doctors to order more expensive tests or discourage them from hospitalizing patients who appear unable to pay for their care. Uncooperative physicians may be threatened with the loss of their hospital privileges.

Recently the hospital industry has experienced a shakedown of sorts. With fewer health care dollars to go around, and the spirit of health care reform in the air, hospital chains are paring down operations in an effort to economize. Hospital industry experts predict that within the next few years hundreds of hospitals will disappear.

The Genesys Health System, a company that operated four hospitals in Genesee County, Michigan, recently decided to replace all four facilities with a single hospital equipped with half as many beds. The company was concerned about dropping hospital occupancy rates. Hospital occupancy rates nationwide dropped from 76 percent to 66 percent between 1981 and 1991 due to a surplus of hospitals.

Genesys also anticipated the introduction of managed competition. Genesys apparently saw the time coming when hospitals and doctors would have to bid against each other for insured groups of patients. Efficient hospital chains offering the highest-quality care at the most reasonable prices will be in the best position to attract patients.[7]

In the Twin Cities of Minneapolis and St. Paul, Minnesota, where about 75 percent of the population is already enrolled in managed care plans, hospitals compete with each other for patients. Six Twin Cities hospitals that lost to the competition were forced to close their doors. The surviving hospitals have had to cut their staffs and inventories. One hospital had to reduce its payroll from 4,000 to 3,500 and reduce its stock of artificial hips from more than twenty-five to three.[8]

And this may be just the beginning. Payments to hospitals are likely to drop with health care reform. This could mean that hospitals will have less money to spend on new medical equipment. Many will follow the example of Johns Hopkins Hospital, which decided to continue using an inexpensive linear accelerator to treat brain tumors instead of purchasing a $3.3 million gamma knife.

I'LL SEE YOU
IN COURT

HOW HAS MALPRACTICE LITIGATION CONTRIBUTED TO THE HEALTH CARE CRISIS?

When the public demands an explanation for the outrageous cost of health care, many doctors cry, "Blame the lawyers." Lawyer bashing is a national pastime, second in popularity only to baseball, perhaps. Lawyers are blamed for everything from the breakup of the American family to rising crime rates. Are lawyers also to blame for the health care crisis?

According to many in the medical profession, lawyers have brought the country to the brink of a health care crisis by encouraging dissatisfied patients to sue their doctors for malpractice. In a malpractice lawsuit, a patient (the plaintiff) accuses a doctor (the defendant) of providing substandard medical care. A plaintiff who successfully proves a doctor's negligence is entitled to damages. Damages are supposed to compensate the plaintiff for medical expenses, lost wages, and pain and suffering. Damage awards in malpractice cases can reach millions of dollars.

To protect themselves against malpractice suits, most doctors purchase malpractice insurance. Doctors covered by malpractice insurance have the security of knowing that, if they are sued, their insurance company will defend the suit. Then, if they lose the suit, the insurance company will pay some or all of their damages (depending on the extent of the doctor's coverage).

Doctors and lawyers hotly debate the contribution malpractice litigation has made to the health care crisis. Each profession has its own side of the story to tell.

Doctors talk about the following statistics, which they argue prove that malpractice litigation is out of control:

•Doctors spend $5 billion to $6 billion a year on malpractice insurance premiums. Hospitals spend closer to $9 billion.[1]
• Since 1978, the number of lawsuits per 100 doctors has gone from 3.3 to 8.9.
•In New York State, there has been a 60 percent increase in the number of malpractice claims filed since 1976, a 232 percent increase in the average size of a malpractice settlement, and a 55 percent increase in the total number of malpractice claims paid.[2]
•One in six obstetricians practicing in New York State have stopped delivering babies out of fear of lawsuits.[3]

In the view of many lawyers, doctors exaggerate the malpractice problem. Lawyers cite statistics showing that the number of medical malpractice claims has actually declined at an average rate of almost 9 percent a year since 1985. They also point out that the billions of dollars spent on insurance premiums represent well under 1 percent of the $800 billion the country spends on health care each year.[4]

Doctors aren't convinced by the lawyers' arguments. They continue to accuse "money-hungry lawyers" of being too quick to sue for malpractice. They claim a trial lawyer will sue a doctor even when there is little or no evidence of malpractice, in the hope of getting *something* from the doctor's insurance company.

Many insurance companies are quick to offer plaintiffs money to settle a malpractice case out of court. The insurers do not want to spend the thousands of dollars necessary to defend the case. Insurance companies would rather give plaintiffs "nuisance money" to make a malpractice case go away than pay the expense of a defense in a trial.

Under the current system of malpractice litigation, patients have just about nothing to lose by suing—and a lot to win. Most malpractice attorneys take their cases on a contingency-fee arrangement. This means they don't collect any legal fees from the client unless they win the case. Plaintiffs don't have to worry about running up huge legal bills and then losing their case, because they only have to pay their lawyer if they win.

Lawyers are willing to assume the risk of a contingency-fee arrangement because they stand to earn major bucks on the malpractice cases they win. The typical lawyer's fee in a malpractice case is one-third of the client's damage award. A client who is awarded $150,000, for example, would pay his attorney $50,000 (one-third of $150,000).

When an insurance company settles a malpractice case without going to trial, the attorney can earn thousands of dollars for just a few hours of work. Cases that go to trial often work out well for plaintiffs and their attorneys, because juries are traditionally very generous when it comes to awarding money to people who sue their doctors for malpractice.

There are probably a few reasons why malpractice juries are so generous to plaintiffs. For one thing, the typical juror probably feels more sympathy for the disgruntled patient, say a parent who must raise a brain damaged child, than for the doctor who was paid thousands of dollars for his services. Jurors may also enjoy playing Robin Hood with health care dollars, taking money out of the pockets of wealthy doctors and returning it to financially strapped patients.

A jury award, however, is a very imperfect way of compensating someone who has been injured by a doctor's negligence. In many cases, there is no way to attach a dollar value to a plaintiff's injuries. For example, how much money would it take to compensate a twenty-three-year-old college football star who loses his leg as a result of a doctor's negligence? Should the patient collect the amount of money he could have earned over the rest of his life if he had two legs? What if he can prove that he stood a good chance of getting a million-dollar contract with a professional football team? Should he then be entitled to a million dollars from the doctor? And what about the emotional trauma of losing a leg? Should he be compensated for that? If yes, how much?

Most medical malpractice awards have three parts: 1) payment of the plaintiff's medical expenses, 2) payment of the plaintiff's lost wages, and 3) compensation for the plaintiff's "pain and suffering." Pain and suffering is the largest part of most medical malpractice settlements. While the first two parts of the award can be estimated with some degree of accuracy, how can any juror assign a value to someone else's pain and suffering?

The inability to calculate objectively the value of someone's pain and suffering is reflected in the lack of uniformity among malpractice awards. The same injury that brings an award of $50,000 from a New York City jury may bring only $10,000 from an upstate New York jury. The amount of money juries award for pain and suffering depends on many factors, including the juror's ethnic background, geographic area, and economic class.

Despite the good living many attorneys make

suing doctors, the legal profession doesn't defend the malpractice system based on its own financial interests. Rather, lawyers claim that malpractice litigation benefits society by disciplining incompetent physicians.

Other than facing the risk of being sued for malpractice, doctors are barely held accountable to the patients they treat. Only 151 of the 4,606 doctors who were the subject of complaints filed with the New York Office of Professional Medical Conduct in 1992 were disciplined. Only a handful of those lost their medical licenses.[5]

And, like the rest of us, doctors are only human. They make mistakes. The AMA has acknowledged that as many as 14 percent of all practicing doctors are drug addicts or alcoholics.[6] Once doctors get a medical license, they don't have to take any tests or attend any lectures on developments in their field to keep their licenses up to date.

However, there is little evidence that malpractice litigation really does protect the public against incompetent physicians. Doctors who are repeatedly sued for negligence and lose do not automatically lose their medical licenses. They are not required to undergo any special training or review, and state licensing boards aren't even aware of the thousands of malpractice cases that settle out of court. Few patients would know if the doctor treating them just lost a million-dollar malpractice suit.

There is even some evidence that the threat of being sued results in *worse* health care for the public. Let's look at the hypothetical case of Susan, a twelve-year-old girl who is brought to the emergency room after falling down a flight of stairs. Susan's doctor doesn't need to X-ray Susan's skull to determine the proper course of treatment, but he orders an X ray anyway. Why? Because if Susan's recovery does not go as expected the doctor wants to be able to testify in a malpractice suit that he performed every available test to diagnose Susan's condition.

This puts Susan at some risk. Prolonged exposure to X rays has been associated with birth defects and cancer. The benefits of the legal protection the doctor gets by ordering the X ray may be outweighed by the risks the X ray poses to Susan.

Doctors claim that they must perform unnecessary tests and medical procedures to protect themselves in the event they are sued. They say they need to be prepared for the patient who claims in court that the medical outcome would have been better if the doctor had run one more test or performed one more procedure.

A doctor who performs excessive medical services solely with an eye toward defending a future malpractice suit practices *defensive medicine*. The AMA estimates that *defensive medicine adds more than $21 billion to the nation's health care bill.*[7]

One of the most common examples of defensive medicine is the caesarean section. A caesarean section (often called a "C-section") is a surgical procedure whereby a fetus is removed from the uterus through a cut in the woman's abdomen. Obstetricians are accused of performing unnecessary C-sections out of fear that vaginal births leave them more open to malpractice claims. A government study found that 349,000 unnecessary C-sections were performed in 1991. Many of these were apparently done out of fear of legal proceedings.[8]

There are two primary problems with the excessive use of C-sections. Cost is the first. The price of a C-section approaches $8,000. The price of a vaginal delivery is closer to $4,000. The second problem is one of quality of care. A C-section is major surgery. The surgeon must make a very deep incision in the woman's abdomen to reach the fetus. This raises the risk of infection, and there is a long recovery period. Vaginal deliveries, on the other hand, pose only minimal risks to the mother. The recovery period is a matter of days. There is even evidence that babies derive a respiratory benefit by passing through the mother's birth canal.

Lawyers have several responses to doctors who support the practice of defensive medicine. The lawyers don't buy the argument that defensive medicine puts doctors in a better position to defend malpractice suits. Why, the lawyers ask, would a doctor be less guilty of negligence just because he or she performed some additional medical services that were not appropriate for the patient's diagnosis or treatment? It doesn't make sense. Skeptical lawyers accuse doctors of creating the myth of defensive medicine to cover up the real reason doctors perform unnecessary medical services: to get more money out of their patients.

Lawyers also dispute doctors' claim that defensive medicine is a significant cause of rising health care costs. They point to the AMA's own findings that defensive medicine accounts for less than 2 percent of the nation's medical spending.[9]

When the defensive-medicine argument doesn't fly, doctors fall back on the high-price-of-malpractice-insurance argument. According to doctors, patients have to pay more for medical care because doctors have to pay such high rates to their malpractice insurance companies. High insurance rates are passed from doctors to patients in the form of increased fees.

There is no question that the cost of malpractice insurance is out of sight. Obstetricians practicing in New York City pay about $100,000 a year for malpractice insurance.[10] Do the lawyers have a response to this argument against malpractice litigation? You bet they do.

Lawyers accuse doctors of exaggerating the impact of insurance premiums, which are responsible for less than 1 percent of the nation's health care costs.[11] They also note that the average premium for physicians in nonmetropolitan areas was $12,400 in 1990, chicken feed compared to their average annual income of $130,500.[12] Finally, they point out that the insurance industry, not the legal profession, is to blame for out-of-sight insurance premiums.

Insurers make lots and lots of money off doctors. Insurers pay out in defense costs and malpractice awards only a fraction of the money they collect in premiums. Profits among malpractice insurance carriers exceeded $110 billion between 1977 and 1987.[13]

Most doctors are willing to admit that lawyers do not bear sole responsibility for the prevalence of malpractice litigation. The deterioration of the doctor-patient relationship has also made it easier for dissatisfied patients to sue their doctors.

In the past, people formed close and trusting relationships with their family doctors over long periods of time. This relationship made patients reluctant to sue for malpractice. Now the doctor-patient relationship is much more fragile because people go to specialists for their basic medical care. Specialists, unlike family doctors, usually see their patients for only a few brief, impersonal visits over a short period of time. This does not foster the same sense of loyalty that patients once developed to their longtime family doctor. Patients also tend to expect more from specialists. When a specialist fails to deliver a medical miracle, patients are quicker to sue.

Another development that many doctors see as contributing to the malpractice crisis is a change in the rules of malpractice litigation. In the past, patients suing for malpractice had to bring in local doctors to testify about the doctor's incompetence. Patients had a hard time finding physicians willing to swear under oath that a colleague provided substandard medical care. Doctors were generally unwilling to testify against one another because they rely on other doctors for referrals of patients. Ear specialists, for example, give the names of ophthalmologists (eye specialists) to their patients who complain of eye trouble. A doctor who testified against another doctor ran the risk of being closed out of the local circle of referrals. Under the revised rules of litigation, patients can use out-of-state medical experts, textbooks, and medical journals in place of live witnesses to establish their doctor's negligence.

Although doctors and lawyers may disagree about their relative responsibility for the health care crisis, most agree that malpractice litigation has changed the practice of medicine in a number of fundamental ways. One such effect is in the doctor-patient relationship which, as we have seen, has already changed over the last few decades.

Doctors and patients have traditionally been bound by a relationship of trust, respect, and concern. Now doctors and patients are increasingly seeing each other as potential adversaries in a future lawsuit. This mistrust understandably causes some doctors to distance themselves from their patients. This distance is troubling for patients who need emotional support, as well as medical care, from their doctors.

Nowhere is this distrust more evident than in Philadelphia, where some doctors pay $80 a month to find out if a prospective patient has ever filed a malpractice suit against another doctor. They pay the money to a service called Courtscan, which will soon be available to doctors in New York, Chicago, Houston, Los Angeles, and Miami.[14]

Malpractice litigation has also inhibited doctors' spirit of experimentation to some extent. Doctors are more likely to stick with tried-and true approaches to treating illness. They are less likely to search for creative solutions to their patients' problems, at the risk of being sued. Although no patient wants to be a human guinea pig, innovative thinking is sometimes necessary to solve unusual or complex medical problems.

Doctors who take an extremely conservative approach to medicine are said to practice "cookbook" medicine. Just as a recipe in a cookbook spells out every step the cook should take when making a soufflé, doctors who practice cookbook medicine follow standard procedures when treating their patients. Cookbook practitioners tend to view their patients as nothing more than a sickness or injury that requires a prescribed course of medical treatment. They disregard the individual needs of each patient.

Other doctors react to the threat of being sued by refusing to treat certain types of medical problems, perform certain procedures, and/or practice medicine in certain areas of the country. Fifty-five percent of the members of the American College of Obstetrics/Gynecology stopped performing high-risk deliveries out of fear of suit, and 18 percent abandoned their obstetrics practice entirely.[15] A survey by the Medical Society of New York showed that 42 percent of New York-trained physicians planned to practice out of state where malpractice premiums and awards are lower.[16]

The unavailability of certain high-risk medical procedures in particular regions of the country is a growing concern. Seriously ill patients must sometimes travel long distances to obtain care, or settle for treatment by unqualified local providers.

A number of proposals for reforming the health care system take aim at malpractice litigation. The New York legislature has proposed the creation of a "no-fault" insurance system that would compensate the families of injured infants without any litigation. The centerpiece of the proposal is a yearly fund of $90 million. Obstetricians (doctors who deliver babies) and hospitals would contribute $300 to the fund each time a baby was born in a New York hospital.

Under the proposal, infants born with injuries that *might* have been caused by a doctor's negligence can receive payments from the fund of several thousand dollars a year, possibly for life, regardless of whether the hospital and/or physician was at fault. In return for this guarantee of compensation, however, the infant's family must give up the right to sue the hospital and doctor for malpractice. *Needless to say, the bill faces steep opposition from New York lawyers.*[17]

Different states are trying different approaches. California imposed caps on jury awards for pain and suffering in 1975 and now boasts some of the lowest malpractice premiums in the country.[18] Other states use checklists that spell out which medical procedures are appropriate for the treatment of which medical conditions. Doctors who follow the guidelines cannot be sued for malpractice.

Federal proposals for reforming the health care system include restrictions on medical malpractice lawsuits and awards. Some of the ideas under consideration include limiting damages for a patient's pain and suffering, reducing a patient's damages by the amount of insurance coverage he or she receives, allowing doctors to pay off malpractice awards over a period of time, and encouraging the out-of-court settlement of malpractice claims. A more radical proposal, called *enterprise liability* would relieve individual doctors of liability for malpractice. Hospitals and health plans that employ doctors would be solely responsible for paying patients' damages.[19]

Not surprisingly, the legal profession vigorously opposes most of these proposals. Why? Because each proposal hits the lawyers below the belt—that is, in the wallet.

THE TEN-DOLLAR
ASPIRIN

WHAT ROLE HAVE PHARMACEUTICAL COMPANIES PLAYED IN
BRINGING ABOUT A HEALTH CARE CRISIS?

*T*he drug industry is under fire. Critics charge drug manufacturers with making huge profits at the expense of the public's health. They cite the following statistics in support of their accusations:

•Drug companies are consistently among the most profitable of all U.S. companies, with profits averaging 14 percent.[1] This represents a rate of more than four times that of the average Fortune 500 company.[2]

•Since 1980, drug prices have risen more than three times as fast as the rate of inflation.[3]

•Over the past ten years, the cost of a full series of recommended vaccinations in a private doctor's office has gone from $23 to $244.[4]

Drug manufacturers have been accused of overpromoting and overpricing their products. This chapter will examine the accuracy of these charges and consider whether drug companies should be faulted for doing what every other American industry tries to do—make money.

First, let's look at the charge that drug manufacturers overprice their products. The question comes down to whether pharmaceutical companies are gouging the public or just trying to make an honest buck for their shareholders.

A drug maker who invents a new product has total freedom to set the price of the new product. More often than not, the manufacturer uses this freedom to set the price of its product as high as the market will bear. The problem is that the market can bear a lot when it comes to prescription drug prices. Market forces don't work to hold down drug prices the way they hold down the cost of other consumer products, because money is often perceived as being no object when the consumer's health is at stake.

Imagine your doctor has just told you that you have a serious medical condition. Left untreated, the condition will result in blindness, paralysis, and then death. The only available treatment is pills that costs $10,000 a year. What are you going to do? *Not* buy the pill to protest its high cost, or run to the pharmacy as fast as your legs can carry you with wads of money in your outstretched hand? How much time do you need to make this decision—one second or two?

What makes the situation even worse is that drug manufacturers that invent new products don't even have to compete with other drug companies for the public's business. Drug inventors can get a lock on the market by applying to the government for patent protection. When a drug inventor's patent application is approved, no other company can manufacture and sell any products that are the same as the patented product for a period of years. Drug inventors say they must recoup the high cost of researching and developing a new drug.

Luckily for the consumer, patent protection doesn't last forever. Most drug patents expire after about twenty years. This is good news, because when a patent terminates other drug companies can put their own version of the drug on the market. This gives the inventing company some competition. Within a year or two after a patent expires, when the competition starts to heat up, sales of major brand name drugs can be cut in half.

However, history shows that drug companies will price their new drugs outrageously high for as long as they can get away with it. The drug company Upjohn lost two valuable patents in 1993, on Xanax, an antianxiety drug, and Halcion, a sleeping pill. These drugs earned Upjohn millions of dollars a year in United States sales. In anticipation of the loss of sales to the competition when the patent protection expired, Upjohn jacked up its prices. The cost of Xanax went up 25 percent between January 1990 and January 1991, and the price of Halcion went up 30 percent.[5]

Market forces don't work to hold down drug prices for the additional reason that the people who decide what drugs to buy aren't the same people who pay for the drugs. Think about it. Doctors control the prescription pad, so in essence *they* decide what drugs people will buy. A patient with an ear infection doesn't decide if she should buy tetracycline or amoxycillin. Her doctor makes that decision. But doctors don' t pay for drugs. Patients do.

Perhaps drug companies would be under greater pressure to hold down their prices if consumers decided which pills would sell and which would sit on the shelf. This is the way the market holds down the cost of other products. Shoppers won't pay $5 for a can of furniture polish when a $3 can does the job just as well. Likewise, a patient wouldn't pay $2 for a pill when a $1 pill would do the trick.

Doctors who prescribe costly drugs are not trying to bankrupt their patients. More likely, they are ignorant about how much the drugs they prescribe cost. Of the thousands of drug ads that appear in medical journals, few mention cost. Drug manufacturers bombard doctors with promotional materials that boast the benefits of their drugs, while conveniently leaving out any mention of the cost.

Drug companies start trying to influence doctors to buy their products while the doctors are still in medical school. They give medical students free pens, pads, calendars, and books imprinted with the names of their drugs. They offer substantial discounts to hospital pharmacies so student interns and residents become familiar with their company's products. Drug companies also make major charitable donations to hospitals. The drug maker Marion Merrell Dow, for example, contributed an undisclosed amount of money to the University of Cincinnati College of Medicine to establish a cardiovascular research center.

When the students become full-fledged doctors, drug makers step up their promotional efforts. They sponsor breakfasts, luncheons, dinners, seminars, conferences, and awards for doctors. They give away free drug samples, slides, and tapes. They entertain at medical conventions and offer all-expenses-paid trips to doctors and their families.

Evidence shows that all of this advertising and promotion by the drug industry works. Doctors are as influenced by the pitch of drug company salespeople and promotional brochures as they are by pharmacological data. They recommend prescription drugs over equally effective over-the-counter drugs, and brand-name drugs over equally effective generic "no-name" drugs.

Doctors' preference for prescription drugs over nonprescription drugs can be seen in the preferred treatment of arthritis. Nuprin and Advil are two over-the-counter brands of arthritis medications. Feldene and Voltaren are two of the best-selling prescription arthritis medications. Daily doses of Feldene and

Voltaren cost about $2. Nuprin and Advil cost substantially less. Although pharmacological data show that most patients find no difference in effectiveness between the two products, doctors continue to prescribe the high-priced prescription medications. In fact, worldwide sales of prescription arthritis drugs approximated $5 billion in 1990.[6]

Doctors also prefer brand-name drugs over generic drugs. Generic drugs, which are discussed in greater depth directly below, are as effective as their brand-name counterparts but cost much less money. Nevertheless, about 28 percent of all prescriptions are filled with higher-priced brand-name products, even when generic versions of the drugs are available.[7]

When a drug patent expires, every pharmaceutical company is free to manufacture its own version of the drug and market it under the drug's generic name. The generic name is the name of the active chemical ingredient in the drug. For example, the active chemical ingredient in the brand-name sedative Valium is diazepam. Diazepam is the generic name for Valium.

Chlorpropamide is a chemical that reduces blood sugar levels in diabetics. Pfizer's brand name for chlorpropamide is Diabinese. In the late 1980s a major national drugstore chain charged $31.54 for 100 tablets of Diabinese. The same chain charged $7.50 for 100 tablets of generic chlorpropamide.[8]

Brand-name drugs cost about 70 percent more than generics. A 1984 report issued by the Federal Trade Commission estimated that generic drugs save consumers about $236 million a year.[9]

Despite the claims brand-name manufacturers make in their promotional materials, generic drugs have been proven to work as well as their brand-name counterparts. Before they can be sold to the public, generic drugs must meet the FDA's strict approval standards. Specifically, makers of generic drugs must prove to the FDA that their products contain the same amount of the same active ingredient found in the brand name version of the drug.

Advertising by drug companies appears to have gone completely out of control. In 1993, the typical drug company was found to spend as much as 20 percent of its budget on promotion. By contrast, most consumer-based industries spend about 2 percent of their budgets on marketing, while some beer and cosmetics companies spend 10 percent or more.

Drug marketing really took off in the 1980s. In that decade, drug makers discovered several new drugs to treat a number of chronic illnesses (illnesses that last for long periods of time). Some of the chronic illnesses that became treatable with prescription drugs included ulcers, high cholesterol, high blood pressure, and arthritis.

Patients with chronic illnesses often must stay on some type of medication for the rest of their lives. High blood pressure, for example, is rarely "cured." It can, however, be controlled with medication and diet. People with high blood pressure spend thousands of dollars over the course of their lives on blood pressure-lowering drugs. This, of course, means a lot of money to the manufacturers of blood pressure pills.

The drug companies began researching promotion. They discovered that if they paid one salesperson to visit forty doctors and the salesperson succeeded in convincing at least one doctor to prescribe a medication to treat at least one of the doctor's chronically ill patients, the salesperson's costs would be covered. Additional sales would mean more profit for the manufacturer.[10]

The number of people selling prescription drugs rose 50 percent in the late 1980s.[11] By 1993, drug companies were spending about $12 billion a year on promotion, more than they were spending on drug research.[12]

In recent years, the FDA and several medical associations have started to regulate what drug companies can and cannot do to promote their products. Drug companies must now reveal their sponsorship of medical lectures and conferences. The 1990 *Code of Pharmaceutical Marketing Practices* prohibits certain "giveaway" programs, where drug companies give doctors free airline tickets, free medical equipment, and/or free drugs in exchange for prescribing their product. Guidelines issued by the American Medical Association discourage doctors from accepting gifts from drug makers that appear to have been made to influence the doctor's medical decisions.[13]

In response to these restrictions, the drug industry has developed more subtle ways of promoting its products. Instead of offering a doctor an outright bribe for prescribing a particular pharmaceutical, a company may hire the doctor as a "consultant" to praise the particular medicine at a medical convention, in a medical journal, or during rounds at a hospital. Drug companies circulate newsletters designed to look like medical journals. The drug company's name doesn't appear on the newsletter, but the company uses the publication to tout the benefits of its drugs.[14]

Extensive advertising by drug manufacturers gives rise to several important concerns. First, there is the issue of affordability. The drug companies' increasingly elaborate promotional schemes have contributed to the rising costs of producing drugs, making them unaffordable to many.

Second, there is the danger of misleading advertising. Drug manufacturers often pressure salespeople to say whatever is necessary to persuade doctors to prescribe their product. This leads many drug salespeople to downplay bad side effects of the drugs and to overstate the benefits and uses of the drugs.

The Food and Drug Administration (FDA) has

stepped up efforts to stop corrupt promotional practices in the pharmaceutical industry. In one such enforcement effort, the FDA sued a New Jersey company that manufactured a drug to treat ulcerative colitis (an illness in which ulcers form on the inside of the bowel). One of the drug's side effects is diarrhea. Since diarrhea is a main symptom of ulcerative colitis, the FDA had only approved the drug for use when the disease is in an inactive phase, and did not approve the drug for use in children at all.

The FDA found evidence that the president of the drug company had instructed his sales force to tell doctors that the drug was good for the treatment of active colitis and for use by children. According to the FDA, such uses of the drug could make patients much worse. To settle the case, the drug company agreed to rewrite its promotional material, retrain its salespeople, start a six-month advertising campaign to reeducate doctors about the drug, and to pay the FDA $85,000 to cover the cost of its investigation.[15]

A related problem is the risk to public health that drug advertising can cause. The whole point of advertising is to create a market for a product, but not everybody who is the target of the advertising campaign will always benefit from the drug. As a result, drug promotion can lead to dangerous and inappropriate overprescribing of a pharmaceutical.

The problem of overprescribing has been around for many years. As early as 1980, only one out of thirty prescriptions of the sedative Valium, for example, was medically necessary. With pharmaceutical companies buying more and more hospitals and physicians' groups and perhaps encouraging their doctors to use their products, the danger that drugs will be overprescribed is heightened. Large drug manufacturers already have substantial ownership interest in several health care corporations, including Humana and the

Hospital Corporation of America. Although there is no proof that physicians who work for companies that are owned in whole or part by drug companies prescribe more medications, the risk is certainly there as there is a clear conflict of interest.

Drug makers follow the same rules of business as other American industries. They make decisions that maximize their profits. They use every means possible to sell their product, beat out their competition, and make as much money as possible. In other words, they take the slogan of American business to heart: *Caveat emptor*, or let the buyer beware.

The problem is compounded when much-needed drugs are priced out of reach of the patients who need them the most. Take, for example, the situation that arose when Burroughs Wellcome began to market AZT, the drug that slows the onset of the symptoms of AIDS. At first, Burroughs Wellcome charged an unaffordable $10,000 a year for AZT. Desperate AIDs sufferers who could not meet this expense waged a media war that finally succeeded in pressuring the company to cut the cost of AZT.[16]

Sandoz, the maker of the schizophrenia drug Clozaril, had a similar experience. Sandoz initially charged $9,000 for a year's supply of Clozaril. Patients who could not afford the drug sued the manufacturer. After defending more than thirty lawsuits, Sandoz reduced the price of Clozaril.[17]

High drug prices hit the elderly especially hard. Medicare does not cover prescription costs. An elderly patient who suffers from congestive heart failure must spend about $200 a month on medications. For an elderly person whose only income is from Social Security, this can quickly become unaffordable. Many older patients must draw on their savings, if they have any, to pay their pharmacy bills.

The drug companies defend high drug prices on

several grounds. They argue that high drug prices are necessary to cover the expense of bringing new pharmaceutical products to the market. Spokespeople for the pharmaceutical industry say that the cost of researching and developing new drugs is sky-high, both in terms of dollars and time. They say it takes over $200 million and twelve years to bring a new drug to the market, from initial testing through FDA approval.[18]

Drug companies also defend their high prices by showing how their products are bargains when compared to the cost of alternative treatment methods. Take, for example, the printed advertisement of the Pharmaceutical Manufacturers Association (PMA): "Ask Mike what he'd do if you took away the ulcer drug that's saving him from a $25,000 operation." In the text of the ad, in much smaller, nonbold print, the advertiser admits that ulcer drugs cost "a sizable $1,000 a year." The PMA clearly counts on the $25,000 figure dwarfing the $1,000 figure.[19]

The Synergen Corporation took this defensive strategy one step further when it hired a staff of "pharmaco-economists" in connection with its introduction of a new costly drug to the market. The pharmaco-economists were told to gather data proving how many health care dollars the system would save by treating patients with the new drug and keeping them out of the hospital. Synergen saw the need to gather ammunition to defend the anticipated $30,000-a-year cost of the new drug per patient.[20]

American drug companies manufacture 42 percent of the major drugs marketed throughout the world.[21] The pharmaceutical industry justifies high drug prices based on the cost of drug research, yet the typical drug company spends more money promoting itself than developing new products. Between 1982 and 1986, only about one-third of the $4.7 billion drug manufacturers earned from price increases was spent developing new drugs. In 1991, pharmaceutical companies spent $1 billion more on advertising than research.[22] In 1993, drug companies were spending 22 cents of every prescription dollar on advertising, and only 16 cents on research.[23]

Drug companies also waste millions of research dollars bringing to the market "me-too" drugs—drugs that the manufacturers claim are better than products already on the market but are really no improvement at all. Only 58 percent of the new drugs brought to the market in the late 1970s and the 1980s provided some benefit over existing drugs. Of the ninety new drugs approved by the FDA in 1992, only about 40 percent were a significant improvement over medicines already available to consumers. A 1993 congressional study found that most of the new versions of drugs already on the market offered no therapeutic advantage over the existing drugs.[24]

Why would a drug company spend millions of dollars developing a blue pill that does essentially the same thing as the yellow pill another company already sells? To remain competitive. No drug company wants to give a competitor a lock on a market. The result is a tremendous waste of research dollars—dollars that are collected from the patients and insurance companies that pay inflated drug prices.

The drug company Wyeth-Ayerst came up with a "new and improved" version of its popular hypertension drug Inderal when competitors started to close in on its market. It called the new product Inderal Long Acting Capsules (Inderal LA). In an aggressive and costly marketing campaign, Wyeth-Ayerst promised doctors who prescribed Inderal LA a free trip anywhere in the United States, Hawaii, or the Caribbean, or free medical equipment and books. All told, Wyeth-Ayerst spent (or wasted) thousands of dollars developing an unneeded drug, and then thousands of dollars more trying to convince doctors and patients that Inderal LA was the only high blood pressure drug to use.[25]

A final problem with the drug industry's reliance on the high-cost-of-medical-research argument in defending high drug prices is that the public already pays for drug research with its tax dollars. The majority of the most important drugs that came on the market in 1990 and 1991 were developed with substantial federal assistance. All but three of the cancer drugs that have come on the market since 1955 were developed with the help of significant federal financing.[26]

The National Institutes of Health (NIH) and other federal organizations distribute billions of tax dollars to private drug researchers each year. The FDA then gives private drug manufacturers the right to manufacture and sell drugs developed with public funds. The FDA considers a number of factors when deciding where in the private market to place a new drug product. Specifically, the FDA looks at how competently and quickly each competing company will be able to manufacture and distribute the new product. The government does *not* consider how much the private drug company intends to charge the public for the drug.

Thirty-two million dollars of public funds were spent bringing Taxol, a new drug to treat ovarian cancer, from the initial testing stage almost through FDA approval. The FDA then granted rights to Taxol to Bristol-Myers Squibb. The fact that Bristol-Myers Squibb planned to charge patients between $4,000 and $6,000 for a year's supply of Taxol was not relevant to the FDA. But consumer advocates argue that this high price is unreasonable in light of the public's already considerable financial investment in Taxol.[27]

Ceredase, a drug used to treat an extremely painful inherited enzyme disorder called Gaucher's disease, was also discovered and developed by researchers and scientists paid with federal funds. The FDA gave the job of manufacturing and marketing Ceredase to Genzyme, a private drug maker in Boston. Genzyme charges patients as much as $300,000 a year for Ceredase. The company defends this high price as necessary to cover the cost of making the drug, but critics argue that the price is excessive.[28]

The Scripps Research Institute (SRI), a large private research laboratory that receives about $70 million a year from the government, was recently reprimanded by the National Institutes of Health (NIH). SRI had entered into an agreement with a Swiss drug manufacturer that gave the manufacturer first rights to all of SRI's future discoveries for $300 million. NIH objected to the agreement, saying that no single drug company should have the exclusive right to profit from discoveries paid for in part with public funds.[29]

In 1989, NIH started urging pharmaceutical companies to charge a "fair" price for drugs that were developed with public funds. The government took this step in response to the public's outrage at the price tag of $10,000 a year per patient Burroughs Wellcome first put on AZT, the primary drug for treating AIDS. AZT was discovered at the National Cancer Institute and was given to Burroughs Wellcome to manufacture and market. The cost of AZT has now dropped to around $3,000 a year.[30]

What's a fair price for drug products developed with government money? Not only doesn't the government have any standards for determining what price is fair, the government also has no way to enforce the fair price requirement. There is even a question whether the NIH has the legal authority to force private companies to set prices that NIH considers fair.

Warner-Lambert has used all of the defense strategies discussed above to justify the anticipated annual cost of Tacrine, a recently invented drug to treat Alzheimer's disease (a brain disorder that slowly destroys tissue, causing loss of memory and reasoning ability). The company has pointed out how much money it spent researching and developing Tacrine and how much money the health care system will save by treating fewer Alzheimer's patients.

Of course, the unspoken reason for Warner-Lambert's charging as much as it can for Tacrine is that the drug maker's primary responsibility is to the shareholders who have invested their money in the company. Warner-Lambert obtained exclusive rights—a patent—to manufacture the only drug available to treat a widespread, and greatly feared, degenerative brain disease. The president of Warner-Lambert is duty bound to take full advantage of the situation to maximize the company's profits.[31]

The United States is now the only industrialized nation that does not regulate drug prices or drug profits. In England, the British government controls drug prices, and this control is reflected in drug prices. A polio vaccine that costs $10 a dose in the United States costs only $1.80 in England.

The only restriction on American drug profits is included in a law that was passed by the United States Congress in 1990. This law requires drug makers to give refunds on prescriptions paid by Medicaid. If a drug manufacturer raises the cost of its drugs faster than the rate of inflation, the amount of the refund goes up. Medicaid is the drug industry's largest customer.

The FDA has started to take cost into consideration when evaluating new drugs. For example, the FDA refused to approve a drug to treat sepsis, a deadly bacterial infection, in part because the drug cost $3,750 a dose.[32] Although the FDA still doesn't rely directly on price in deciding whether or not to approve a new drug, a panel of scientists that helps the FDA evaluate new therapies has begun to take cost into consideration.

The federal government took another small step toward reining in drug profits when it passed legislation guaranteeing free vaccines to millions of poor and uninsured children. Under the program, drug companies must sell vaccines to the government at discount prices. Doctors who participate in the program then receive the vaccines at no charge, and do not charge their patients for the vaccine. Not surprisingly, drug manufacturers strongly opposed the legislation. The chairman of one drug company warned that the free vaccine program "could be the death knell for future research in developing new vaccines."[33]

Most drug companies also have programs to provide drugs free or at reduced cost to the poor. Pfizer, one of the most successful drug companies, has the largest such program. Under the program, Pfizer makes eleven drug products available at no cost to 500,000 to 1 million uninsured Americans. The drugs are distributed through community health centers that provide medical care in low-income communities across the country. The cost to Pfizer of the program in its first year was about $10 million, compared to Pfizer's annual sales revenue of $4.5 billion.[34]

A number of proposals for reforming the health care system include price controls on pharmaceutical products. The proposal that has been taken most seriously by the Clinton Administration recommends establishing a drug price review board. The board would use production costs and other data to establish guidelines for reasonable drug prices. The board would then use the media to blast companies that violated the guidelines. In theory, the fear of bad press would pressure drug makers to keep their prices within the guidelines.

Not surprisingly, drug manufacturers strongly oppose the idea of a price review board. They worry that their confidential research, production, and marketing information will become public knowledge. They also warn that research into new drugs will be stopped dead in its tracks if price controls are instituted.

In an effort to avoid government-imposed cost controls, the pharmaceutical industry agreed in 1992 to voluntarily limit its price increases. Drug prices rose only 50 percent over inflation in 1992.[35] Although this is the lowest increase in fifteen years, drug increases were still four times the increase for other products.[36] Even when compared to other high-risk, high-tech, research-intensive industries, drug company profits were still "excessive" according to a 1993 government report.[37]

There is evidence that voluntary limits on price increases will not do the trick. While members of the Pharmaceutical Manufacturers Association agreed to hold price increases to the cost of living, nineteen of the thirty-one largest drug manufacturers that pledged not to raise prices faster than the rate of inflation were found by a Senate committee actually to have raised their prices more than double the rate of inflation. Voluntary limits on price increases also leave drug manufacturers free to set any price they want for new drugs.[38]

There are two other proposals for restraining drug prices that also have drug manufacturers quaking in their corporate boots. One proposal would require drug companies to offer elderly Medicare beneficiaries the same discounted prices on pharmaceuticals the companies have been required to offer low-income Medicaid beneficiaries since 1988. With Medicaid and Medicare beneficiaries accounting for half of all prescription drug consumers, the extension of the discounts would have a noticeable impact on drug company profits.[39]

The second proposal would authorize the Secretary of Health and Human Services to deny Medicare coverage for any drug she considered too expensive. This proposal raises the disturbing picture of the government denying Medicare coverage to an elderly beneficiary who desperately needs a high-priced patented drug. Drug prices might fall with this law, but the costs in terms of human health and compassion might be too steep.

Experts on health care reform predict that drug prices will start to come down even without price controls if and when managed competition takes hold in the United States. The Pharmaceutical Manufacturers Association favors managed competition over outright price controls. (See chapter 9.) Skeptics don't believe managed competition will work to control drug prices, because they don't see any room for bargaining and competition when only one drug manufacturer produces a drug the public needs.

Chapter Seven

WILL THAT BE CASH OR CHECK?

IS THE GREED OF HEALTH CARE PROVIDERS RESPONSIBLE FOR AMERICA'S STATE OF CRISIS?

*H*ow do you feel about the medical profession? Do you respect doctors and admire the job they do healing the sick and comforting the dying? Or do you think most physicians are more concerned with how much money they make than with ministering to their patients' needs?

If you are like 60 percent of people polled, you blame doctors for some or most of the health care crisis. Eighty-one percent of the public think doctors charge too much.[1]

Many Americans are surprised to learn that only 20 percent of the billions of dollars they spend each year on health care goes toward doctors' fees.[2] If doctors aren't profiting from the public's health care spending, why does the medical profession have such an image problem?

The answer may lie in the cultural and economic gap between the typical doctor and the typical patient. Most doctors are white, male, and come from families at the top of the American economy. To make matters worse, these "privileged" doctors earn about six times the salary of the average worker.[3]

These characteristics, which do not reflect the makeup of society in general, lead many people to conclude that doctors are just in it for the money. But aren't most workers in their jobs for the money? How many secretaries would go to the office each day, and how many packers would go to the loading dock each day, if they weren't getting paid? Not many, that's for sure.

So why are doctors criticized for making a living from their profession? After all, doctors invest up to ten years of their lives, and many thousands of dollars, in their medical education, and then work between forty and sixty hours a week. Aren't they entitled to compensation for their efforts?

Many people think not. They hold medical professionals to a different standard than other workers. They see medicine as a profession that people should enter only if they want to serve society, not to make oodles of money and drive Mercedeses and Porsches. Doctors, like teachers and priests, are expected to be motivated by human compassion, not the almighty dollar sign.

The perception of doctors as money-hungry is fed by the growing number of physicians who become medical specialists. Specialists earn far more money than general doctors. While general physicians provide patients with less advanced treatment for a wide variety of medical conditions, specialists undergo extra training in particular procedures and illnesses.

The salaries of medical specialists are impressive: radiologists earn an average of $229,800 a year, obstetricians/gynecologists bring home about $221,800, anesthesiologists make around $221,100, and cardiovascular surgeons in group practice average about $500,000. Compare these salaries to that of a general practitioner, who earns a relatively measly $111,500, or a pediatrician, who only makes about $119,300.[4]

The percentage of doctors entering general medicine has dropped steadily since 1960. Only 25 percent of 1987 medical school graduates entered primary care. By 1990, only about 33 percent of all practicing physicians were in primary care.[5] By the year 2010, the number is expected to be as low as 28 percent or less.[6]

Some health care economists say that, in an ideal health care system, 50 percent of all doctors are general physicians.[7] Out of 600,000 physicians practicing in the United States today, 400,000 are specialists.[8] Half of the doctors in this country will not be in general practice until 2004, even if every single medical school graduate from 1993 on goes into general medicine.[9]

The shortage of family doctors has hit the rural areas of the country particularly hard. Huge regions of the country have no doctors at all, because specialists tend to practice in big cities.[10] The shortage of primary-care physicians has also put a strain on the U.S. health care system. General practitioners hold down health care costs by performing fewer costly tests and procedures, and referring only patients who have especially complex medical conditions to high-priced specialists. Someone who goes to a specialist for basic medical care pays the specialist's high fees.

Medical students often justify their entry into well-paying specialties by pointing to the huge amount of debt they accumulate during medical school. The typical medical school graduate must pay off about $55,000 in student debt.[11] Most new doctors don't start earning enough money to repay their student loans until four or five years after graduation. During the first year of a residency, a medical school graduate earns about $28,618. By the third year of the residency, his or her salary may go up to $31,795. Many doctors feel they deserve the high salaries of specialists after they put in four years as a hardworking student and three or more years as a low-paid resident.

To encourage more medical students to go into primary care, the federal government now offers low-interest loans to medical students who promise to enter general practice upon graduation.[12] Many hospitals and health care plans have also started offering family practitioners and internists bonuses and higher salaries to attract more primary-care providers.

General physicians and specialists alike have traditionally been paid on a fee-for-service basis. The more services they provided, the more money they got paid. The medical profession's use of this payment system has not done anything to help its reputation. Doctors paid on a fee-for-service basis have been found to perform more medical services than physicians who are paid the same salary regardless of how many procedures they perform. One study found fee-for-service doctors ordering 50 percent more electrocardiograms and 40 percent more X rays than salaried doctors. These statistics raise the obvious question of whether these additional tests are medically necessary or are prescribed by doctors looking for an easy way to make an extra buck.[13]

The evidence is against the doctors. Between 30 and 50 percent of all medical tests and operations have been found to be inappropriate.[14]

Hopefully, the problem of excessive medical care will be less of a concern after health care reform. With the establishment of large numbers of managed-care plans, more doctors will be salaried employees. (See chapter 9.) Their income will stay the same no matter how many medical services they provide. They will no longer stand to make more money by performing more tests and procedures.

Other reform efforts designed to limit doctors' earnings rely on price controls. Many price control proposals are modeled on the federal Medicare program (the public health insurance program for the elderly). Since January 1, 1992, the federal Medicare agency uses fee schedules to set payment rates for doctors and hospitals that treat Medicare beneficiaries.

The Medicare fee schedule used to pay doctors is called a *relative-value scale*. It assigns a value unit to a variety of medical services. More time consuming and complex medical services receive a higher value unit. Simpler medical services receive a lower value unit. Health care providers who perform medical services with higher value units receive larger Medicare payments.

For example, under the Medicare program the government assigns a regular office visit 1.00 value unit. In 1993, each value unit was worth $31.25 to the provider. Every time a Medicare beneficiary saw a doctor for a regular office visit, the government paid the doctor $31.25. This payment stayed the same regardless of how much the doctor charged his or her non-Medicare patients.

An X ray, which requires less time and expertise than an office examination, is assigned only 0.77 value unit on the Medicare fee schedule. This lower value unit corresponds to a payment of $24.06. A CAT scan, which is a more sophisticated test than an X ray, has 9.31 value units, which translates into a Medicare payment of $290.94.

To reimburse hospitals, Medicare uses another fee schedule called Diagnosis-Related Groups (DRGs). DRGs are categories of medical conditions. There are 487 DRGs. Medicare has assigned a fee to each DRG that is supposed to reflect the average cost of treating the conditions in the DRG. When a Medicare beneficiary enters the hospital, the government fits the diagnosis into a DRG Medicare then pays the hospital based on the appropriate DRG, not the actual cost to the hospital of treating the patient. Unfortunately, the hospitals purchase software which, based on diagnosis codes, etc., indicates to the hospital which DRG will get the highest reimbursement.

Some reform proposals recommended extending

Medicare's relative-value and DRG fee schedules to private insurance companies and consumers. Under these proposals a doctor could not charge more than $31.25 for an office visit, whether the patient was insured by the John Hancock Insurance Company or was using his own money to pay his bill.

The idea behind these proposals is to prevent doctors from charging privately insured and private-pay patients higher fees to make up for the money they claim they lose treating Medicare patients. Such higher fees have forced insurance companies to raise their rates and have made health care unaffordable for many private-pay patients.

Not surprisingly, the American Medical Association (AMA) opposes reform proposals that limit doctors' freedom to set their own fees. This opposition has political significance, because the AMA has earned considerable influence over members of Congress by making generous contributions to their election campaigns. Between 1981 and 1991, the AMA gave almost $12 million in congressional contributions.[15] During the 1991–1992 congressional races alone, the AMA contributed almost $3 million.[16] Legislators who receive these funds often use their votes to demonstrate their loyalty to the medical profession.

Lawyers for the AMA have even argued that price controls violate the Fifth Amendment of the Constitution. They base their argument on the constitutional provision that prohibits the government from taking private property "without just compensation." Lawyers for the doctors argue that this clause prevents the government from interfering with a doctor's right to benefit from the investment made in a medical career.

Finally, the medical profession argues that price controls would do more harm than good. They say capping the incomes of health care providers would drive talented people out of the profession, weaken physicians' commitment to the practice of medicine and soon disable the entire health care system.

Hospitals and doctors that treat Medicare beneficiaries have found a number of creative ways to avoid Medicare's fee schedules. For example, under the DRG schedule Medicare pays hospitals $8,000 for each appendectomy they perform on Medicare beneficiaries. Many hospitals get around the $8,000 payment cap by farming out some of the surgical work to private physicians who must be paid separately. The hospital may hire a private anesthesiologist to sedate the Medicare patient, a private pathologist to test the patient's samples, and a private radiologist to read the patient's X rays. Suddenly the $8,000 Medicare payment doesn't cover the full cost of the operation. There are anesthesiology, pathology, and radiology bills that must also be paid.

Another way hospitals get around Medicare's restrictive payment system is to shift part of the cost of treating Medicare beneficiaries to non-Medicare patients. Medicare may pay a hospital only $500 for a medical procedure that costs the hospital $750 to perform. To make up for the shortfall, the hospital will bill a non-Medicare patient $1,000 for the same procedure (to cover the $750 cost of performing the procedure plus an extra $250 to make up for the money lost on the Medicare patient). This practice is called cost shifting. However, if Medicare payments were more generous, the hospitals might still charge high amounts to non-Medicare patients.

As a result of cost shifting, insurance companies pay more than their share of hospital costs. Not only do they pay for the hospital services that are provided to the patients they insure, they also help pay the cost of providing hospital care to Medicare beneficiaries and other uninsured and underinsured patients.[17] In 1990, as a result of cost shifting privately insured patients paid 28 percent more than their share of hospital costs.[18]

What would happen to cost shifting if price controls are imposed throughout the health care system? Hospitals would no longer be able to make up for the money they "lost" treating Medicare beneficiaries because the fees paid by privately insured patients would also be capped. Would hospitals have to "eat" the loss?

Probably not. What is more likely to happen is that hospitals would find other ways to avoid the price controls. Doctors, who can' t use cost shifting as easily as hospitals to avoid Medicare price controls, have found other creative ways to avoid the government's relative-value fee schedules.

Three of the most innovative ways doctors have found to avoid Medicare's price controls are to *overtreat* their patients, *upcode* their claims, and *unbundle* their services. Each of these tactics is discussed below. Doctors learn these and other techniques for maximizing their income at "creative billing" seminars.

With overtreating, doctors provide their Medicare patients with extra tests and procedures. The doctors figure they will make up for the money they lose to low reimbursement rates by submitting more reimbursement claims. The more Medicare claims the doctors submit, the more money they collect from the government.

Other doctors get around Medicare fee caps by billing their patients for services that pay higher reimbursement rates. This practice is commonly known as upcoding.

Finally, some physicians boost their bills by breaking down each medical procedure into several parts, a practice called unbundling. Unbundling is best explained with an example. Medicare pays $2,900 for a gastrectomy (the removal of all or part of the stomach).

A surgeon who submits a single claim for a gastrecto-my will receive a $2,900 check from Medicare. But a surgeon who submits several separate claims for each part of a gastrectomy, from the insertion of the IV tube through the closure of the incision, can get as much as $7,000 from Medicare.[19] Unbundling earns doctors bundles of money.

America's complaints about the medical profes-sion are not limited to the high fees doctors and hospi-tals charge. The public is also concerned about physi-cians who exploit the health care system for their own financial gain. Medicaid fraud, for example, is estimat-ed to account for as much as $80 to $100 billion of annual U.S. health care spending.[20]

Fraud appears to run especially rampant in the blood-testing industry. Federal authorities expanded their investigation into the entire industry after National Health Labs (NHL), a large California blood-testing company, pled guilty to filing $111.4 million of false claims to Medicare and Medicaid. Employees for the laboratory defended their actions on the ground that overcharging was common practice in the blood-testing business. The company was eventually ordered to repay the federal and state agencies for the over-charges.

In other scams, doctors and dentists give their patients inflated bills so their patients receive larger reimbursement checks from their insurers and the doc-tors get paid more for their services. Hospitals and doctors have even been known to submit claims to insurance companies for services that were never pro-vided. Four out of ten customers of the Aetna Life and Casualty insurance company said their doctors had cheated insurance companies.[21]

A prime example of an unethical practice that is common among doctors, and that costs health care consumers millions of dollars a year, is self-referrals—when doctors send their patients to laboratories, surgical centers, and/or rehabilitation clinics in which the doctors have a financial interest.

Patients who go to facilities owned by their doctors, on the advice of those same doctors, fatten their doctors' wallets. With self-referral, the patient can never be sure her doctor is sending her for tests because they are medically necessary or because they bring money to a lab the doctor partly owns.

Physicians with financial interests in businesses related to their medical practices have, in fact, been found to "overrefer" their patients for tests and procedures. In Miami, where doctors own 93 percent of the diagnostic imaging centers, 78 percent of the radiation therapy centers, 60 percent of the clinical laboratories, and 38 percent of the rehabilitation centers, imaging scans and some lab tests are prescribed twice as often as in Baltimore, where few doctors own such facilities.[22]

Researchers in Arizona also found that doctors who owned diagnostic imaging equipment ordered four times as many exams as doctors who referred their patients elsewhere for testing. A 1989 study conducted by the Inspector General of the Federal Department of Health and Human Services found that patients of doctors with a financial interest in diagnostic laboratories were referred for 45 percent more tests than other patients.[23]

Doctors stand to make a lot of money by investing in testing equipment and facilities. An orthopedist who invests $100,000 in an MRI scanner earns back his investment after referring only 100 patients for scans (or should we say "scams"?).

To stem the problem of overreferral, in 1988 the federal government started barring doctors from owning laboratories that treated Medicare or Medicaid patients. Three years later, some states (including New York and Florida) prohibited doctors from investing in some patient services, including X ray and imaging centers and clinical labs. Illinois has passed the broadest legislation to date, banning doctors' investments in any services to which the doctors refer their patients.

In 1992 the AMA ruled that most physician self-referrals were unethical, and called on members to sell their financial interests in medical facilities to which they refer patients. The AMA statement, while not legally binding, has stigmatized the practice of self-referral. The AMA's Council on Ethical and Judicial Affairs has recommended that, at the very least, doctors should disclose their investments in testing centers and laboratories to their patients, and give their patients the names of alternative facilities.

Some doctors who have been discouraged from investing in laboratories and clinics have put their money instead into home-care. In increasing numbers, doctors are investing in companies that provide medical equipment, services, and medications to patients who are recovering from illnesses and injuries at home. There are no current estimates of the number of doctors who have money invested in the home-care industry. However, one of the largest home-care companies did disclose that 2,200 doctors invested in their operations in 1992, up from 650 doctor-investors in 1988. A federal study found that 25 percent of the companies that provide intravenous drug and nutrition treatments in the home to Medicare and Medicaid patients include doctors among their investors.[24]

Home-care investing yields generous returns for doctors. A typical investor in T2 Medical, one of the largest home-care companies, puts up $100 in cash. That $100 investment can earn the doctor over $20,000 in a single year.[25] Not bad.

Many doctors are lured into the home-care industry by national home-care companies that travel the country looking for investors. The companies promise to help the doctors in the area set up a local home-care agency. The national company agrees to manage the agency in exchange for a percentage of the agency's profits (usually 25 percent or less). The rest of the agency's profits go to the doctor-owners.

For the most part, this type of home-care investing is legal, as long as the services don't involve Medicare or Medicaid reimbursement.[26] The federal government is, however, investigating a kickback scheme involving two of the largest home-care companies, T2 Medical and Caremark International. As of January 1994, the Inspector General of the United States was investigating whether the companies paid doctors to refer patients to their agencies.[27]

Critics of the ties between medical professionals and home-care companies point out that doctors with a financial interest in a particular home-care agency will always refer their patients to that agency. Once that agency has a lock on a source of referrals, there is less competition in the home-care industry. Without competition, prices can more easily rise, and quality of care can more easily fall. Home-care companies respond that patients receive better care when doctors own the agency.

Doctors who invest in home-care say the AMA's existing statement disapproving of physician self-referrals does not apply to them. They rely on the exclusion in the statement for referrals to services that are a "direct extension" of the referring doctor's practice. Home-care services, they argue, are a "direct extension" of the referring doctor's practice, because the referring doctor oversees the services their patients receive at home. Laboratory services, on the other hand, are not a direct extension of the referring doctor's practice because independent nurses and lab technicians provide the services.

The AMA has responded that its statement on self-referrals was intended to oppose any arrangement that nets doctors huge amounts of money on very small investments. The AMA is considering rewriting its statement to explicitly cover doctors' investments in home-care.

Although the medical profession's reputation may be in some trouble now, this has not always been the case. For more than a century, physicians have been among the most revered members of society—and understandably so. After all, doctors have the capacity to prescribe that magic pill, ointment, or therapy that relieves pain, lifts depression, or saves a life.

When disease was thought to be a form of punishment from God, physicians in some societies were viewed as godlike healers. Many of the first physicians were actually priests, trained in both religion and medicine. They cured patients by helping the patients make peace with God.

In many primitive cultures, the tie between religion and medicine still exists. The shaman and the Navajo medicine man use both psychic and physical means to heal their patients. Religious ceremonies are employed to cast out devils and summon God, and herbs, chemicals, and surgical procedures are used to diagnose and treat illness and disease.

Many doctors long for the recent past. They want to regain the public's respect and reestablish close and trusting relationships with their patients. This explains, in part, beneficial actions by the AMA, including a new acceptance of some type of health care reform.

Toward this end, some medical schools and hospitals are teaching new doctors how to improve their bedside manner. They offer classes in which actors play the role of patients in various medical situations. In one class, an actress may pretend to be a patient dying of cancer. The doctor must gently explain to her what she can expect in her final days, and provide her with emotional support.[28]

This type of sensitivity training is supposed to

bring back the old-fashioned hand-holding doctor who knew how to listen to patients. There is hope that the return of this breed of doctor will decrease health care costs. More patients may obey their doctors' orders, and fewer patients may sue their doctors for malpractice.

Doctors who have joined an organization called Doctors of the World are doing their part to polish the reputation of the medical profession. They provide free care to people around the world who lack access to basic medical services. The organization sends doctors to underdeveloped nations such as Somalia and Ethiopia, and arranges for volunteers to operate clinics in some of America's poorest neighborhoods.

One such clinic operates in the South Bronx, where large numbers of residents suffer from AIDS, drug addiction, alcoholism, and other serious illnesses. Volunteers with Doctors of the World staff a makeshift clinic whose only equipment is a box of rubber gloves and syringes. No examining table. No X-ray machine. No blood pressure machine.[29]

Many of the patients who visit the Doctors of the World clinic in the South Bronx have not seen a physician for years. Others have received all of their medical care from overcrowded hospital emergency rooms, where they wait up to ten hours to be examined by a doctor they never see again.

If more doctors made similar efforts to earn the public's respect and admiration, the medical profession's reputation would soon be shining brightly.

Chapter Eight

AND COVERAGE FOR ALL

WOULD THE CANADIAN SYSTEM OF NATIONAL HEALTH INSURANCE WORK IN THE UNITED STATES?

*I*n Canada, almost all of the nation's medical bills are paid by the government, using tax dollars. Virtually every citizen gets health insurance from the government, and every doctor accepts insurance payments from the government. This makes Canada a single-payer health care system, with the government being the single payer of most of the country's health care expenses.

The U.S. health care system is a far cry from a single-payer system. Here hundreds of insurance companies, thousands of private individuals, fifty state governments, and a huge federal bureaucracy pay for the country's health care. The U.S. health care system is a "many-payer" system, not a single-payer system.

Some of the promised benefits of a single-payer health care system are reduced administrative costs, universal coverage, cost control, and increased efficiency. Each of these benefits is considered below.

First, let's look at efficiency (or lack thereof, in the case of the U.S. health care system). The amount of time and money wasted each year administering America's health-care system's fifteen hundred different health insurance programs is mind-boggling.[1] Medical offices across the country spend hundreds of thousands of dollars a year paying administrators and clerks to learn and follow the complex rules and procedures of the different insurance companies. Doctors, nurses, and hospitals must take valuable time out of each workday to complete insurance claim forms, call insurance adjusters, and follow up on outstanding insurance claims. All of this billing-related paperwork consumes massive amounts of time and money.

And the situation only gets worse when public medical benefit programs are taken into account. Under the Medicare and Medicaid programs, the government pays the medical bills of the elderly and the disabled (Medicare) and the poor (Medicaid). The rules governing *private* insurance companies are as simple as ABC compared to the rules that govern public insurance programs. Detailed Medicare and Medicaid regulations are set out in thousands of pages of tiny, single-spaced print in volumes and volumes of government publications. Scores of lawyers get paid six-figure salaries to advise health care providers on how to comply with this mass of technical rules.

Thanks to the simplicity of a single-payer system administrative costs are far lower in Canada. When a Canadian patient sees her doctor, she gives the receptionist a plastic card with a magnetic stripe on it. The receptionist runs the card through a machine to register the patient's government-assigned health care number. The Canadian government is then billed directly for the patient's care. Neither the patient nor the doctor ever fills out a claim form or sees a bill.

In Canada, about 11 cents of every health care dollar goes toward administrative costs.[2] (Critics contend that there are hidden adminisrative costs in the Canadian system that are not included.) In some parts of the U.S., administrative costs account for between 20 cents and 25 cents of every health care dollar.[3] The billing department of a 240-bed Canadian hospital is staffed with three employees. A typical 240-bed New York hospital employs forty full-time workers in its billing department. According to the General Accounting Office, the United States could save $67 million in administrative costs alone by adopting a Canadian-style health care system.[4]

Administrative waste is not the only type of waste that plagues the U.S. health care system. This country also wastes valuable medical resources, another problem the Canadian system avoids. One small town in Pennsylvania, for example, has three magnetic imaging resonance (MRI) machines, each costing over $1.5 million. Although the local population is far too small to support the need for three MRI scanners, the two hospitals and one medical group in the area purchased the equipment to compete with one another for the limited pool of prospective patients.

Now patients in and around this Pennsylvania town receive MRI scans in record numbers. Why? Because doctors in the area prescribe MRI scans for everything from headaches to joint pain. The only losers in the competition among providers turned out to be the patients who receive unnecessary MRI scans and the health care system that pays for them.

The situation in California is equally troublesome. Each of California's 110 hospitals is equipped to perform open heart surgery. The problem is that not enough California residents suffer from heart problems (if that can be called a problem). As a result, many of the state's hospitals perform heart surgery less than once a week.[5]

The Canadian system cuts down on wasted medical resources through centralized control. The government, by paying most hospital bills, controls most hospital budgets. This puts the government in a good position to say which hospitals will buy which medical equipment, and which won't. By withholding funds, the government, in theory, can keep the wasteful duplication of costly medical equipment to a minimum.

In addition to minimizing waste, the Canadian system also boasts an ability to control medical inflation. Canada uses fee schedules and a national health care budget to hold down health care spending.

With price controls, doctors and hospitals get paid a set amount for each medical test and procedure they perform. A surgeon in Ontario, for example, gets paid $190 for each appendectomy. Surgeons in America get paid between $3,000 and $4,000 for the same procedure.[6]

Price controls have apparently worked to hold down doctors'salaries in Canada. While the typical Canadian physician earned just over $100,000 in 1990, the average U.S. doctor earned about $165,000 that same year.[7]

Canada has also taken several steps to hold down costs associated with malpractice litigation. (See chapter 5.) Canada caps awards for pain and suffering. Some Canadian provinces also prohibit lawyers from taking malpractice cases on a contingency fee arrangement so patients have to pay their lawyers' money up front. This discourages many patients from suing.

Finally, frivolous malpractice suits are kept to a minimum in Canada, because the organization that represents most Canadian doctors aggressively defends every case. Canadian patients with weak cases against their doctors have trouble finding representation, because lawyers know they can't count on a quick settlement from an insurance company.

Canada seems to have succeeded in holding down costs associated with malpractice litigation. The average malpractice premium for a U.S. physician in 1987 was $15,000. For a Canadian physician, the bill came to only $1,470.[8]

There is evidence that the U.S. malpractice system could benefit from some of the changes that have been adopted in Canada. As stated in chapter 5, in America, money for pain and suffering makes up the largest chunk of most malpractice awards, the contingency system makes suing for malpractice almost risk free for the plaintiff, and insurance companies are quick to settle even frivolous malpractice lawsuits to save legal defense costs.

The Canadian health care system is also designed to hold down the cost of prescription drugs. In 1987 Canada established a Patented Medicine Prices Review Board. The board investigates drug prices, gets confidential price information from drug companies, and withdraws the patent rights of drug companies that fail to comply with the board's requests to reduce excessive prices. (In Canada, a drug price is "excessive" if it costs more than comparable drugs and treatments.) The Canadian government, as the number one purchaser of pharmaceuticals in the country, also forces drug companies to lower their drug prices by boycotting (not buying) overpriced products.[9]

In the United States, the cost of prescription drugs has risen at rates several times higher than the consumer price index. A comparison of 121 drugs revealed that drug manufacturers price most of their products higher in the United States than in Canada. In 1991, five of the most commonly prescribed drugs cost between 5 and 183 percent more in the United States than in Canada.[10]

American drug makers claim that any comparison between drug prices in the United States and Canada is misleading. Drug prices have to be higher in America, they argue, to cover the high cost of researching and developing new drugs. The Canadian drug industry, unlike the American drug industry, produces few important new drugs.

In fact, however, the Canadian review board for drugs succeeded in getting drug companies to hold down prices while increasing their spending on research, according to a U.S. government report. The report suggests that the United States could benefit from a Canadian-type drug price review board.[11]

Perhaps the biggest bonus of the Canadian system is universal health care coverage. Every Canadian resident is covered under a public health insurance plan that pays for a wide range of medical services with only small out-of-pocket expense to the patient. The coverage is the same whether the resident is rich or poor, working or unemployed.

If the Canadian system is so great, you might wonder, why doesn't the U.S. government adopt it lock, stock, and barrel? Good question. Even though 69 percent of Americans surveyed said they would favor adopting a Canadian-style single-payer health care system,[12] the U.S. Congress is unlikely to pass national health insurance legislation for political reasons. The million dollar American insurance industry hates national health insurance. There is no need for the private health insurance industry if people can get comprehensive health insurance for free from the government.

Politics isn't the only reason national health insurance is unlikely to come to America any time soon. A closer look at the Canadian system reveals some significant flaws. For one thing, statistics comparing health care spending in the U.S. and Canada are deceptive. While it is true that each Canadian citizen consumed only $2,110 of government health care dollars in 1991, while each U.S. citizen spent $2,817,[13] the Canadian figure excludes the costs of dental care, prescription drugs, ambulance service, private hospital rooms, many cosmetic procedures (such as face-lifts and tummy tucks), and glasses. Many Canadians purchase private insurance (the cost of which is not included in the government's figures) in addition to their government insurance to cover these costs. All of these expenses are included in the U.S. figure.

Also, the cost of Canadian health care is rising. Health care spending in Canada has begun to outpace the availability of tax dollars. The Canadian government used to use taxes to pay half of the nation's health care costs. Now taxes cover only 30 percent of the nation's health care spending.

The Canadian government has had to start requiring citizens and employers to pick up more of their health care tab. For example, Canadians now have to pay $19.80 toward the cost of a throat culture. In the twenty-seven-year history of the Canadian universal health insurance system, residents were never asked to dip into their own pockets to pay for common medical services.[14]

How can health care costs be rising in Canada when the Canadian government regulates hospital budgets and doctors' fees? The most likely explanation is twofold: an oversupply of doctors, and the fee-for-service payment system.

Canada has too many doctors. Today there is approximately one doctor for every 450 Canadians; in 1964, there was one doctor for every 800 Canadians. The added competition means there are fewer patients to go around. Each new Canadian doctor costs the local government $500,000 a year.[15] Since Canadian doctors are paid on a fee-for-service basis, the more medical services they provide the more money they get paid. With fewer patients to go around, doctors must provide the patients they have with more medical services.

Canadian doctors have been able to get away with overtreating their patients because the Canadian government has traditionally avoided questioning doctors' treatment decisions. However, more recently the Canadian government has started taking steps to address the population explosion that has occurred within the medical profession.

At the government's urging, the University of

Toronto medical school reduced its enrollment by 30 percent. Fee schedules were also revised to punish doctors who provide excessive medical services. For example, the government now pays a doctor $41.50 for a house call, instead of the customary $71, when more than 20 percent of the doctor's billings are for house calls. A doctor who earns over $400,000 a year also receives reduced payments.[16]

A comparison of United States and Canadian health care spending is also misleading because the U.S. has more elderly people, more drug abusers, and more pregnant teenagers than Canada. The United States *should* be spending more on health care than its neighbor to the north to meet the needs of these populations. About 10 percent of the annual increase in U.S. health care spending went to caring for people over 65.[17] Abortions add another $1 billion or so a year to the U.S. health care bill. Treatment of substance abusers adds still more.

Critics of the Canadian health care system also raise questions about quality of care. American doctors are better trained than Canadian doctors. More than 60 percent of American physicians are highly trained specialists, while less than 50 percent of Canadian physicians are specialists.[18] There is no question that American doctors run rings around Canadian doctors when it comes to advanced medical training, but there's also no question that America pays dearly for its large number of specialists. Specialists charge higher fees than less skilled generalists. With more and more Americans going to specialists, the cost of health care goes up.

Another aspect of the quality of care issue is the scarcity of advanced technological products in Canadian hospitals and medical institutions. A survey of Canadian doctors found that half of those polled complained of a lack of well-equipped medical facilities; only 14 percent of U.S. doctors cited this as a problem. New York City, with a population of 7.3 million, has 1,171 kidney dialysis units; there are only 325 such units in Ontario, Canada, with a population of 11 million.[19]

Americans also receive more medical services than Canadians. Waiting lists for operations, which are common in Canada, are almost unheard of here. In some parts of Canada, patients have to wait up to eighteen months for hip replacement surgery and six months for coronary bypass surgery. In 1990, fifteen Canadians on a waiting list for heart surgery died while waiting to be scheduled for surgery. A patient may have to wait six weeks for a CAT scan, a high-tech form of X ray that is commonly used to detect the spread of cancer.[20]

Canadians respond that there may not be waiting lists in America, but there are inequities surrounding who gets medical care and who doesn't. For example, it's true that 80 percent more bypass operations are performed in California than Canada, but it's also true that the rate of bypass surgery in California is higher in the richer neighborhoods than the poor. In Canada the opposite is true, which makes sense because heart disease is more common among the poor. At least in Canada, rich and poor alike are put on waiting lists for heart surgery.

Finally, opponents of the Canadian-style national health-insurance system warn that such a system would result in higher taxes. Canada has already found it difficult to raise enough public funds to finance the continually rising cost of health care. With the U.S. debt already in the trillions of dollars, any reform proposal that is likely to cause broad-based tax increases is virtually doomed.

Chapter Nine

MANAGING MANAGED COMPETITION

IS COMPETITION AMONG PROVIDERS AND INSURERS THE ANSWER TO THE NATION'S HEALTH CARE CRISIS?

What in the world is managed competition? Boxing matches and spelling bees that are kept under control? Not quite. Managed competition is a type of health care system that is based on managed care. Managed care is a general term that describes any network of doctors and hospitals. The earliest form of managed care was the health maintenance organization (HMO). Since HMOs are still the most popular form of managed care, the following discussion of managed care focuses on HMOs.

An HMO is defined as a "prepaid group practice health-care plan." Let's look at each part of this definition separately.

Prepaid: An HMO is called a prepaid health plan because people who join an HMO pay for their health care ahead of time—before they receive any medical services. They pay a set fee at the beginning of the month, and are entitled to all the medical care they need for the rest of the month at little or no extra cost.

An HMO may, for example, charge each member a $200 monthly fee. After paying the $200 fee, the member receives whatever medical services he or she requires that month for no additional money. A healthy HMO enrollee who doesn't cough or blow his nose all month doesn't get a refund of the $200 fee, and an unhealthy member who requires triple bypass surgery during the month doesn't have to pay anything extra.

Because members of an HMO pay the same monthly fee whether they are sick or well, HMOs try to keep their members healthy. They promote good health by providing their members with preventive care —health care that keeps people from getting sick. Vaccinations, an annual physical exam, and nutritional counseling are all examples of preventive care. For members of most HMOs, these types of services are provided as part of their monthly fee.

Under the traditional fee-for-service payment system, patients pay for their medical care when they receive the care. After a patient sees his doctor, for example, he gives the doctor's receptionist a check for the cost of the visit on his way out the door. HMO patients who prepay their medical expenses with their monthly fee don't have to pay any medical bills when they see their doctors. At most, they have to pay their doctor a small co-payment (rarely more than $10) at the time of each visit.

Group practice: An HMO is defined as a group practice because each HMO has a network of doctors, specialists, hospitals, clinics, and laboratories that are connected with the plan. The HMO pays these health care providers to treat the members of the HMO. In fact, HMO members are *required* to receive their health care services from the doctors, hospitals, labs, and providers that are connected with the plan.

Each HMO distributes to its members a directory of its health care providers. Members that receive care from providers outside the plan must pay for the care with their own money (except for emergency care). The monthly fee the member pays to the HMO does not cover the member for care provided by *non-*

network health care personnel. This is quite a departure from the traditional health care system, which permits people to pick their own doctors—by asking friends for recommendations, by choosing among the physician listings in the telephone book, or by any other method.

HMO enrollees pick a primary-care doctor from the directory of HMO network physicians. The primary-care doctor calls the shots when it comes to treating the HMO patient. The primary-care doctor decides what health care the member will receive, whether the member will enter the hospital, how long the patient will stay in the hospital, and whether the patient will see a specialist. HMOs do not permit their members to receive the costly services of specialists and hospitals without first getting permission from their primary-care doctor. You can see why the HMO primary-care doctor is called the gatekeeper of the managed-care system.

Patients outside an HMO are free to see specialists whenever they want, and enter the hospital whenever they think they need inpatient care. They do not have to get prior approval from their primary-care doctor, or anyone else for that matter. A patient seeking treatment of a sprained leg outside an HMO, for example, might go to an orthopedist and pay a $300 fee. The same patient in an HMO would be seen for this condition by a less skilled, and lower paid, general practitioner. Similarly, a patient seeking treatment of chest pain outside an HMO might go to a hospital to be evaluated for admission. The same patient in an HMO would first be monitored for a few days on an outpatient basis.

Health-care plan: An HMO is an entire system, or plan, for receiving health care. A person who joins an HMO knows that all of his or her basic health care needs will be met by the HMO. In the past, the most popular health care plan was the comprehensive insurance policy. A person who bought a good policy knew all of his or her basic health care needs would be paid for by the insurer.

The trend in health care plans is away from traditional insurance coverage and toward coverage in an HMO (or any managed-care plan). There are several explanations for this trend. The primary explanation is that comprehensive health insurance has become unaffordable for many people. These people need an alternative health care plan.

Cost of insurance is not a big concern of people who get their health insurance through work, but employees of small businesses, self-employed workers, and the unemployed are in a different situation. They have to shop for insurance coverage on their own. More often than not, they end up with the short end of the stick. Insurance companies charge them top dollar for poor coverage. The difference between the large corporate consumers of insurance and the small individual insurance consumers is the difference between buying wholesale and retail. Let's look at this analogy more closely.

Insurance companies love to sell insurance to large employers. They drool at the prospect of selling insurance to General Motors, for example. When General Motors picks an insurance company, that company makes big bucks selling thousands of policies that insure thousands of GM workers. This motivates insurers to offer large consumers reduced prices in an effort to beat out the other insurance companies competing for GM's business. The insurers can afford to lower their prices because they stand to sell so many policies. And beyond administrative savings from large groups, they also involve less risk to the insurer.

When it comes to individual workers, however, insurance prices are strictly retail. Insurance companies don't discount their prices because they won't be making up the income they lose in reduced premiums by making large numbers of sales. They also don't care so much about losing the business of a few small customers by charging top prices.

Membership in an HMO is a good alternative health care plan for people who have been priced out of the private insurance market. The monthly cost of joining an HMO is almost always well below the average monthly insurance premium for equally comprehensive coverage.

HMOs hold down their costs by relying heavily on general practitioners. HMO members go to their general physician for all of their basic medical needs, and only members with complicated medical conditions requiring advanced medical expertise are referred to more costly specialists.

HMOs also limit health care spending by controlling hospital stays as much as possible. HMOs instruct their primary-care physicians to refer patients for hospitalization only if absolutely necessary, and to keep the period of hospitalization to a minimum. Some HMOs even penalize doctors who refer too many patients to specialists and hospitals. An HMO will typically withhold between 15 and 20 percent of a doctor's salary as a penalty for excessive referrals.

Managed-care plans also attempt to hold down their costs by limiting the incomes of the doctors they employ. Most physicians employed by a managed-care plan, such as an HMO, get paid in one of three ways: Salary, capitation, or fee schedules. Each of these payment methods is discussed below.

Doctors who are salaried employees of an HMO get paid every week or two like any other salaried employee. The amount of the paycheck stays the same each pay period, regardless of the number of patients the doctors see and the number of medical procedures the doctors perform.

Doctors paid by salary have no incentive to

overtreat their patients. Unlike doctors paid on a fee-for-service basis, salaried doctors don't earn more money by performing more medical services. An HMO doctor gets paid the same salary whether he spends three hours giving a patient complaining of headaches five tests to diagnose the cause of the pain, or tells the patient to take two aspirin and call him in the morning.

Some HMOs with salaried doctors offer year-end bonuses if the health plan makes money. In the years that the HMO collects more money in monthly premiums than it spends on patient care, doctors share the profits. The purpose of the year-end bonus is to encourage doctors to treat their patients as cost effectively as possible, but the obvious danger is that doctors will *undertreat* their patients to save the HMO money. A doctor may be reluctant to prescribe a $1,000 MRI scan if the test might cost the doctor his year-end bonus.

With capitation, another payment method, HMOs pay their doctors according to the number and type of patients the doctors enroll. For each patient the doctor enrolls, the HMO pays the doctor a sum of money calculated to cover the expected cost of treating the patient. For example, an HMO doctor may be paid $1,000 a year for every twenty-five-year-old patient he enrolls because the anticipated cost of treating a twenty-five-year-old is $1,000 a year. The same doctor may be paid $10,000 for every sixty-five-year old patient he enrolls because the expected cost of treating an aging sixty-five-year-old is about ten times the anticipated cost of treating a healthy twenty-five-year-old.

Like the salaried payment method, capitation payments are designed to encourage doctors to hold down the costs of treating their patients. The doctor who gets paid $1,000 a year for a twenty-five-year-old patient better not spend more than $1,000 treating the patient or he'll lose money. In fact, if the doctor provides his twenty-five-year-old patient with only $800 a year of medical care, he can pocket the $200 difference. Doctors paid by capitation are subject to the same temptation as salaried doctors: to scrimp on the care they give their patients.

The fee schedule is the final method HMOs use to pay their providers. Doctors paid under a fee schedule receive a specified sum of money for each medical service they provide. The fee schedule may, for example, provide that each HMO doctor will be paid $50 for giving a physical examination. The payment rate stays the same whether the doctor spends ten minutes or two hours performing the physical examination.

This payment method is most like the traditional fee-for-service payment method, where doctors get paid for each medical test or procedure. The only difference is that the doctors' fees are capped under the fee schedules. Doctors who are not employed by a managed-care plan are free to set their fees as high or as low as they want.

Cost is not the only reason HMOs threaten to replace traditional insurance as the health care plan of choice. More and more Americans are uninsurable. In other words, they can't purchase health insurance at any reasonable cost.

Insurance companies have become increasingly selective about who they insure. Many insurers now separate healthy members of a group from unhealthy members, and cover only the healthy members. This practice is called cherry picking because people with health problems are picked over by the insurance companies.

HMOs don't engage in cherry picking. As a general rule, they are more willing than traditional insurance companies to make coverage available to unhealthy members of small groups and to individuals. That's not to say that every HMO accepts every applicant for membership. Some HMOs refuse to accept groups of applicants that are likely to rake up high medical expenses. An HMO may, for example, refuse to enroll hospital employees. Hospital employees have the reputation of incurring large medical bills because they demand the most advanced and costly medical equipment and drugs. However an HMO will *not* accept a group and then refuse to cover individual members of the group who pose bad health risks. An HMO will not, for example, offer to enroll a clothing manufacturer but refuse to cover the manufacturer's seamstress who has cancer or the assembler who has AIDs.

What role does managed care play in a system of managed competition? Managed competition relies heavily on HMOs and other managed-care plans.

As already mentioned, small groups and individuals have always been the big losers when it came to buying insurance. They didn't have the bargaining power they needed to force insurers to offer them favorable terms on their insurance contracts. Insurance companies tended to offer these consumers "take it or leave it" deals. Small employers and individuals either had to pay a lot of money for insurance policies with inadequate coverage or risk financial ruin by going uninsured. Most took whatever the insurance companies offered them and paid whatever prices the insurance companies charged.

The goal of managed competition is to level the playing field of insurance companies and the small businesses and individuals that buy insurance from them. This can be accomplished through the establishment of health care alliances. The theory behind health care alliances is that there is strength in numbers.

In President Clinton's vision of managed competition, the health care alliances would be government-sponsored groups of consumers. Small health care consumers would join forces in an alliance so the alliance could negotiate with health care plans on behalf of the consumers for the highest-quality coverage at the lowest possible cost. The alliances would comparison shop for health care coverage for their members, who would be primarily small businesses, part-time workers, self-employed individuals, and the unemployed.

Managed-care plans (including HMOs) as well as traditional insurance companies would compete for the business of the alliances. Since each alliance would represent large numbers of health care consumers, these providers would now be eager to negotiate with the alliances in order to win their business. The alliances would give small businesses and individuals what they've always needed: the power to bargain with competing insurance companies and managed-care plans for the best-priced, best-quality health coverage.

Large employers would have the option of joining a government- sponsored alliance or forming their own health care alliance. If they formed their own alliance, they would negotiate with health care providers directly on behalf of their employees Large companies that already had the purchasing power to force insurers and managed-care plans to compete for their business wouldn't need the clout of an alliance. (Fee-for-Service plans would also be allowed.)

Every health care plan that competed for the business of the alliances would have to provide a minimum package of benefits, that would include doctors' fees, hospital care, emergency room services, ambulances, lab tests, prescription drugs, periodic physical exams, pregnancy-related services, childhood immunizations, well-baby care, cholesterol screening, and cancer testing. Members of an alliance who wanted to purchase coverage in addition to the minimum package of benefits, say for sex-change surgery or private-duty nursing, would have to pay an additional monthly fee.

A national health board is also part of the president's managed competition proposal. The board would pass national standards of care, monitor competing health care plans, and publish "report cards" evaluating the quality of care of various plans and providers. The report cards would rate each plan on such criteria as patient satisfaction ("What is the average wait for an appointment?"), access to services ("What percentage of members are screened for cholesterol?"), frequency of care ("How many hysterectomies have been performed?"), quality of care ("How many psychiatric patients are rehospitalized after treatment?"), and financial stability ("What is the plan's profit margin?").[1]

Although a national system of managed competition is not yet a reality, managed competition has been attempted on a smaller scale. Xerox Corporation, for example, already uses managed competition to force HMOs to compete for the company's business. In 1993 sixty HMOs agreed to limit their price increases for Xerox employees to an average of only 5.5 percent, well below the increases faced by smaller employers. Competing health care plans have proven their willingness to do what it takes to sign up Xerox's 50,000-plus employees.[2]

The Florida legislature also recently took a chance with managed competition in a last-ditch effort to address the state's growing health care crisis. Health care spending in Florida had gone from $9.4 billion in 1980 to $38 billion in 1992. Two and a half million Florida residents lacked any insurance coverage. Small businesses were being driven out of Florida by the skyrocketing cost of health care, and with small businesses accounting for 95 percent of all Florida jobs the losses were intolerable.

The Florida legislature created eleven health care alliances called Community Health Purchasing Alliances (CHPAs). The job of the CHPAs is to help small business owners and individuals negotiate for the best health care coverage at the cheapest prices.[3]

California has also successfully employed managed competition. More than 875,000 state and local government workers and their families belong to a health care alliance called Calpers. Calpers negotiates with insurance companies and health care plans to purchase $1.4 billion worth of health care for its members.

There is clear evidence that Calpers has the bargaining power it needs to obtain favorable insurance terms for its members. In 1992, twenty of the insurance companies that cover Calpers members held premium increases to an average of 3.1 percent, whereas the statewide average premium increase was 13.2 percent the same year. In 1993, premiums for Calpers members increased an average of only 1.5 percent. Calpers pressures competing HMOs to cut out waste and keep down costs. When one HMO competing for Calpers's business insisted on increasing its premiums more than 10 percent, Calpers withdrew its members.[4]

Tough bargaining by Calpers has had a trickle-down effect. Insurance companies competing for Calpers's business now pressure hospitals and doctors to reduce their administrative costs, eliminate unnecessary care, and lower their rates.

Managed competition is not without its critics. There are concerns about what managed competition will do to the doctor-patient relationship. Under managed care, doctors are no longer solely accountable to their patients. They also have to account to the health care plan that employs them. They must obtain prior approval to perform many tests and procedures, and must hold down the costs of treating their patients.

Americans are also reluctant to give up their cherished right to freely select their doctors. As mentioned above, enrollees in managed-care plans must receive their medical care from a limited selection of doctors in the plan's network, or pay extra.

Small insurance companies don't like managed competition, which they believe will force them out of business. The need for private insurance coverage drops under managed competition, because more people receive all of their health care through their managed-care plan. Large insurers, unlike the smaller companies, like managed competition because they are large enough to establish managed-care plans of their own.

Managed competition has divided the insurance industry. The five largest insurers (Prudential, Cigna, Aetna, Travelers, and Metropolitan Life) have broken away from the insurance industry's established lobbying organization, the Health Insurance Association of America (HIAA). While the HIAA continues to represent small insurers in lobbying against managed competition, the large insurers have formed their own lobbying group to push for managed competition.[5]

Managed care and managed competition also make many doctors uncomfortable. They fear that their incomes will drop as the fee-for-service payment system is replaced by salaries, fee schedules, and capitation payments, and their prestige and independence will decline as they become employees of health care plans.

Will managed competition succeed in meeting the ambitious goals of health care reformers? Whatever the uncertain future holds, one thing is clear—reform of the American system of health care is an idea whose time has come.

SOURCE NOTES

CHAPTER ONE

1. Janice Castro, "Condition Critical," *Time*, November 25, 1991, 32.

2. Marilyn Milloy, "Reform's Battle Lines," *Newsday*, April 25, 1993, 7.

3. Robert Pear, "34.7 Million Lack Health Insurance," *New York Times*, December 19, 1991, B17.

4. Barbara Ehrenreich, "Our Health-Care Disgrace," *Time*, December 10, 1990, 112.

5. Castro, 32.

6. Ibid., 36.

7. Pear, B17.

8. Ehrenreich, 112.

9. Glenn Kessler, "Bitter Medicine," *Newsday*, April 11, 1993, 45.

10. Ibid.

11. "Carter Announces Vaccination Plan," *New York Times*, March 13, 1993, L7.

12. "Our Children at Risk," aired on Public Broadcasting System, November 1, 1991.

13. Ibid.

14. Kessler, 45.

15. Robert Pear, "Health Care Costs Up Sharply Again, Posing New Threat," *New York Times*, January 5, 1993, A1.

16. Harry S. Margolis, ed., "Economic Implications of Rising Health Care Costs," Congressional Budget Office study reported in *The Elder Law Report*, November 1992, 7.

CHAPTER TWO

1. Glenn Kessler, "Bitter Medicine," *Newsday*, April 11, 1992, 43.

2. Study conducted by the Rand Corporation in the late 1970s; Ibid., 44.

3. Elisabeth Rosenthal, "Confusion and Error are Rife in Hospital Billing Practices," *New York Times*, January 27, 1993, C16.

4. Ibid.

5. According to the Health Insurance Association of America, a trade group for private health insurers, employers pay more than seventy percent of all private-insurance premiums; Robert Pear, "34.7 Million Lack Health Insurance," *New York Times*, December 19, 1991, B17.

6. Results of a 1991 poll; Erik Eckholm, "Health Benefits Found to Deter Job Switching," *New York Times*, September 26, 1991, A1.

7. Milt Freudenheim, "The Xerox Health-Care Model," *New York Times*, February 16, 1993, D1.

8. Kessler, 43.

9. Labor Department study; Ibid., 44.

10. "Health Insurance Horror," editorial, *New York Times*, November 16, 1992, A16.

11. Gina Kolata, "The New Insurance Practice: Dividing Sick from Well," *New York Times*, March 4, 1992, A1.

12. Studies by Families USA, a Washington-based advocacy group; William Lowther, "Medicare to the Rescue," *McLean's*, January 13, 1992, 32.

13. Peter Kerr, "Changes Would Transform Worlds of Doctors, Hospitals, and Insurers," *New York Times*, September 11, 1993, 10.

14. Lowther, 32.

15. Adam Clymer, "Clinton Health Plan Aims to Cover Periodic Checkups," *New York Times*, September 1, 1993, A10.

16. University of California, Berkley, Wellness Letter, quoted in *Vitality*, August 1993, 8.

17. Clymer, A10.

18. Mark Bricklin, "Why Our Health-Care System Is Doomed," *Prevention*, August 1991, 29.

19. Ibid.

20. "Insurers Cover New Care," *New York Times*, August 1, 1993, Business section, 2.

21. Tom Morganthau with Mary Hager, Rich Thomas, and Eleanor Clift, "Down to Brass Tacks," *Newsweek*, May 17, 1993, 37.

22. "Our Children at Risk," aired on the Public Broadcasting System on November 1, 1991.

23. A 1993 national study by the University of Rochester, reported in *Newsday*, July 29, 1992, 41.

24. Lowther, 32.

25. Eric Eckholm, "Double Sword for President," *New York Times*, August 23, 1993, A1.

26. According to a survey conducted by the Health Insurance Association of America; Dena Bunis, "Health Care Paradise?," *Newsday*, April 18, 1993, 47.

27. B. Drummond Ayres, "As U.S. Policy Makers Debate, States Move Ahead on Health Care Reform," *New York Times*, April 25, 1993, 30.

28. Elisabeth Rosenthal, "Insurers Second-Guess Doctors, Provoking Debate Over Savings," *New York Times*, January 24, 1993, A1.

29. Ibid.

30. Janice Castro, "Condition: Critical," *Time*, November 25, 1991, 42.

31. Robert Pear, "Health Industry Is Moving to Form Service Networks," *New York Times*, August 21, 1993, A1.

32. Michael Bobrow and Julia Thomas, "In Health Care, Reform Means Rebuild," *New York Times*, July 25, 1993, 13.

33. Kevin Sack, "Cuomo Wants Cap on Doctors' Fees, Private and Public," *New York* Times, March 29, 1993, A1.

34. Marilyn Milloy, "Reform's Battle Lines," *Newsday*, April 25, 1993, 53. A study by the national consumer group Citizen Action found that during the 1991-92 congressional races the National Association of Life Underwriters contributed $1,348,600, the Independent Insurance Agents of America gave $581,098, and the American Council of Life Insurance kicked in $577,430. Associated Press, "Health Industry in Generous Mood," *Newsday*, September 13, 1993, 17.

35. Milloy, 53.

CHAPTER THREE

1. Elisabeth Rosenthal, "Exploring the Murky World of Drug Prices," *New York Times*, March 28, 1993, sec. 4, 1.

2. Elisabeth Rosenthal, "Questions Raised on New Technique for Appendectomy," *New York Times*, September 14, 1993, C3.

3. Robert Pear, "Health Plan Would Use Medicare to Penalize Excessive Drug Prices," *New York Times*, September 10, 1993, A17.

4. Warren E. Leary, "Study Finds Waste in Ultrasound Use," *New York Times*, September 16, 1993, A17; Associated Press, "Fetal Scan Hit," *Newsday*, September 16, 1993, 6.

5. Fazlor Rahman, "Let's Hear It for Low-Tech Medicine," *New York Times*, April 18, 1993, 11.

6. Roni Rabin, "'Free' System Has Its Price," *Newsday*, April 19, 1993, 23.

7. Ibid.

8. Erik Eckholm, "Those Who Pay Health Costs Think About Drawing Lines," *New York Times*, March 28, 1993, sec. 4, 1.

9. Peter Passell, "The Danger of Declaring War on Doctors," *New York Times*, March 21, 1993, 5.

10. "Some Helpful Advice from Five Health Experts," *Money*, July 1991, 77.

11. Jane E. Brody, "Doctors Admit Ignoring Dying Patients' Wishes," *New York Times*, January 14, 1993, A18.

12. Associated Press, "MDs, Nurses: Ease Pain of the Dying," *Newsday*, January 19, 1993, 61.

13. Americans' life expectancy reached a record 75.5 years in 1991. Associated Press, "Americans Living a Bit Longer," *Newsday*, September 1, 1993, 4.

14. Quote from Senator William Cohen of Maine, ranking Republican on the Senate Special Committee on Aging. "Long-Term Care for All," L.A. Times article reprinted in *Newsday*, May 19, 1993, 19.

15. Peter Kerr, "Elderly Care: The Insurers' Role," *New York Times*, March 16, 1993, 19.

16. Jane E. Brody, "7 Deadly Sins of Living Linked to Illness as Well as Mortality," *New York Times*, May 12, 1993, B8.

17. Robert W. Figlesski and Michael A. Harrison, "The Best Health Plan Is Prevention," *Newsday*, February 2, 1993, 37.

18. Brody, B8.

19. Ibid.

20. "Rise in Health-Care Costs Is Linked to Social Behavior," *New York Times*, February 23, 1993, C3.

21. Ibid.

22. Ibid.

23. Article published in the Journal of the American Medical Association; Associated Press, "Alcohol Illnesses Cited as Big Cost," *New York Times*, September 12, 1993, 41.

24. Glenn Kessler, "Bitter Medicine," *Newsday*, April 11, 1992, 44.

25. Ibid.

26. Catherine Woodard, "The Price of Life," *Newsday*, April 12, 1993, 22.

27. A study by the national consumer group Citizen Action found that manufacturers made $745,000 in congressional contributions in the first six months of 1993; Associated Press, "Health Industry in Generous Mood," *Newsday*, September 13, 1993, 17.

28. 1987 study conducted by the Federal Agency for Health Care Policy and Research; Kessler, 44.

29. Robert Pear, "White House Expeced to Back Oregon's Health-Care Rationing," *New York Times*, March 18, 1993, A1.

30. When the new plan goes into effect in January 1994 every Oregon resident with income below the federal poverty level ($11,187 for a family of three in 1992) will get Medicaid; fewer than half of the poor people in most states get Medicaid because the income limits in those states are below poverty level.

31. Kinsey Wilson, "Nobody Likes the R-Word," *Newsday*, April 22, 1993, 45.

32. Katti Gray, "Operating with a Dilemma," *Newsday*, August 20, 1993, 3.

33. Associated Press, "Woman Gets Artificial Heart; First Such Implant in 2 Years," *New York Times*, January 13 and 21, 1993, A7.

34. Dr. Bruce Burlington, the Food and Drug Adminsitration's chief of the Center for Medical Devices; Philip J. Hilts, "FDA to Toughen Testing of Devices," *New York Times*, March 5, 1993, A18.

35. Ibid.

36. Lisa Belkin, "New Wave in Health Care: Visits by Video," *New York Times*, July 15, 1993, A1.

37. 1990 study by the Congressional Budget Office; Kessler, 45.

38. Study published in the Journal of the American Medical Association; "Transplants Studied," *Newsday*, September 15, 1993, 16.

39. Earl Lane, "Stagnation in Health Care Seen," *Newsday*, February 26, 1993, 4.

40. Tim Hilchey, "Two Studies Report Heart Care Lags for Blacks," *New York Times*, August 26, 1993, B8.

41. Congressional Budget Office 1990 study; Kessler, 45.

CHAPTER FOUR

1. For a more in-depth discussion of the issues raised in this chapter, and source of uncited statistics, see Dave Lindorff, *Marketplace Medicine* (New York: Bantam, 1992).

2. Lee Smith, "The Coming Health Care Shakeout," *Fortune*, May 17, 1993, 70.

3. Ibid.

4. Milt Freudenheim, "Merger Proposal to Create Largest U.S. Hospital Chain," *New York Times*, June 10, 1993, D1.

5. Milt Freudenheim, "Physicians Are Selling Practices to Companies as Changes Loom," *New York Times*, September 1, 1993, A1.

6. Ibid.

7. Milt Freudenheim, "Hospitals Begin Streamlining for a New World in Health Care," *New York Times*, June 20, 1993, F12.

8. Smith, 71.

CHAPTER FIVE

1. Estimates made by the American Medical Association and Public Citizen's Congress Watch, a consumer's group; William Falk, "Doctors Divided on Rx," *Newsday*, April 26, 1993, 23.

2. Henry Gilgoff, "Malpractice Insurance Cost Seen Rising," *Newsday*, March 30, 1993, 37.

3. "This Baby's Not Ready to Deliver," editorial, *Newsday*, May 9, 1993, 3.

4. Study by Public Citizen's Congress Watch; Falk, 23.

5. "This Baby's Not Ready to Deliver," 3.

6. Harvey F. Wachsman, "Medical Malpractice Is the Problem Now Lawsuits," *Brooklyn Barrister*, 93.

7. Janice Castro, "Condition: Critical," *Time*, November 25, 1991, 41.

8. Associated Press, "U.S. Says 349,000 Caesareans in 1991 Were Not Necessary," *New York Times*, April 23, 1993, Ai6.

9. Falk, 23; Glenn Kessler, "Bitter Medicine," *Newsday*, April 11, 1993, 43.

10. "This Baby's Not Ready to Deliver," 3.

11. Kessler, 43.

12. Andrew J. Simons, "Health Care Reform: Don't Tamper with the Legal System," *Nassau Lawyer*, April 1993, 24.

13. Ibid.

14. Tamar Lewin, "Philadelphia Doctors to Be Offered Data on Patients Who Have Sued," *New York Times*, August 27, 1993, A21.

15. Robert Emmet Long, ed. *The Crisis in Health Care* (New York: H.W. Wilson, 1991), 53.

16. "This Baby's Not Ready to Deliver," 3.

17. Sarah Lyall, "Cuomo Proposes a Fund for Injured Newborns," *New York Times*, April 21, 1993, B1.

18. Castro, 41.

19. Marilyn Milloy, "A Malpractice Twist," *Newsday*, May 21, 1993.

CHAPTER SIX

1. Catherine Woodard, "The Price of Life," *Newsweek*, April 12, 1993, 23.

2. Richard Berke, "President Assails 'Shocking' Prices of Drug Industry," *New York Times*, February 13, 1993, A1; Brian O'Reilly, "Drugmakers," Fortune, July 29, 1991, 48.

3. Michael Unger, "Vaccine Companies Talk Price," *Newsday*, February 17, 1993, 33.

4. "U.S. Program to Offer Free Vaccine to Poor Children," *New York Times*, August 16, 1993, A15.

5. Cynthia Cotts, "The Pushers in the Suites," *The Nation*, August 31 - September 7, 1992, 20; O'Reilly, 48.

6. O'Reilly, 48.

7. David Pryor, "Drugs Must Be Made Affordable," *New York Times*, March 7, 1993, 13.

8. "The Big Lie About Generic Drugs," *Consumer Reports*, August 1987, 482.

9. James Baker with Mary Hager, "Not What the Doctor Ordered," *Newsweek*, August 28, 1989, 32; "The Big Lie About Generic Drugs," 480.

10. O'Reilly, 54.

11. Ibid.

12. Philip J. Hilts, "Court Bans Impropriety in Promoting a Drug," *New York Times*, August 3, 1993, C5.

13. Michael Unger, "Fraud Case Is Settled by Drug Firm," *Newsday*, July 31, 1993, 14.

14. Alexander Kippen, "Doctored Results," *The Washington Monthly*, October 1990, 38.

15. Hilts, C5.

16. O'Reilly, 48.

17. Ibid.

18. Ibid.

19. *New York Times Magazine*, September 5, 1993, 23.

20. Lawrence M. Fisher, "New Standard for Drugmakers: Proving the Cure Is Worth the Cost," *New York Times*, January 18, 1993, A1.

21. Christine Gorman, "The Price of Life," *Time*, January 8, 1990, 57; O'Reilly, 50.

22. Woodard, 23.

23. Pryor, 13.

24. Ibid.

25. Kippen, 40.

26. A study conducted by the Center for the Study of Responsive Law; Gina Kolata, "U.S. Asked to Control Prices of Drugs It Develops," *New York Times*, April 25, 1993, 36.

27. Michael Unger, "Drug Research Funding Questioned," *Newsday*, February 10, 1993, 39.

28. Pryor, 13.

29. Philip J. Hilts, "Research Group's Tie to Drugmaker Is Questioned," *New York Times*, June 18, 1993, A24.

30. Kolata, 36.

31. Associated Press, "Alzheimer's Drug Approved by FDA," *New York Times*, September 10, 1993, 3.

32. Fisher, A1.

33. "U.S. Program to Offer Free Vaccine to Poor Children," A15.

34. Associated Press, "Company to Give Medicine to Uninsured Poor," *New York Times*, August 15, 1993, L27.

35. Philip J. Hilts, "U.S. Study of Drugmakers Criticizes 'Excess Profits,'" *New York Times*, February 26, 1993, D1.

36. Spokespeople for the Pharmaceutical Manufacturers Association; Woodard, 23.

37. Philip J. Hilts, "U.S. Study of Drugmakers

Criticizes 'Excess Profits,'" *New York Times*, February 26, 1993, D1.

38. Dena Bunis, "Senator Says Drug Firms Broke Pledge on Pricing," *Newsday*, February 4, 1993, 43.

39. Robert Pear, "Health Plan Would Use Medicare to Penalize Excessive Drug Prices," *New York Times*, September 10, 1993, A17; Dena Bunis and Marilyn Milloy, "Health Plan Eyes Private Sector," *Newsday*, September 11, 1993, 9.

CHAPTER SEVEN

1. The Gallup Organization interviewed 755 adults by telephone on March 25-26, 1993; Melvin Kenner, M.D., "We Are Not the Enemy," *Newsweek*, April 5, 1993, 41.

2. According to the American Medical Association; William Falk, "Doctors Divided on Rx," *Newsday*, April 26, 1993, 23.

3. American Medical Association and National Medical Association study; Ibid.

4. Some figures are from the American Medical Association; Ibid.; Other figures come from a study conducted by the Medical Group Management Association.; *Consumer Reports*, July 1992, 444.

5. Roni Rabin, "'Free' System Has Its Price," *Newsweek*, April 19, 1993, 25.

6. *Consumer Reports*, July 1992, 445.

7. According to the Council on Graduate Medical Education, a group authorized by Congress to assess physician supply trends; Combined News Services, "Medical School Applicants at Record High," *Newsday*, September 1, 1993, 17.

8. Elisabeth Rosenthal, "Medicine Suffers as Fewer Doctors Join Front Lines," *New York Times*, May 24, 1993, A1.

9. Combined News Services, 17.

10. Eighteen counties in Texas alone have no doctors at all; Janice Castro, "Condition: Critical," *Time*, November 25, 1991, 39.

11. Combined News Services, 17.

12. Castro, 39.

13. Ibid.

14. Rand Corporation study; Glenn Kessler, "Bitter Medicine," *Newsday*, April 11, 1993, 44.

15. According to a study conducted by Common Cause; Falk, 22.

16. Marilyn Milloy, "Reform's Battle Lines," *Newsday*, April 25, 1993, 53.

17. In 1981 the average hospital lost $3.2 million, including $1.4 million on charity cases, $1 million on Medicare, $745,000 on Medicaid, and $37,000 on other underfinanced government programs; Milt Freudenheim, "Companies' Costs: How Much Is Fair?" *New York Times*, January 7, 1992, D2.

18. A 1990 study of hospitals by the Congressional Budget Office; Kessler, 44.

19. *Consumer Reports*, July 1992, 445; Castro, 40.

20. Milt Freudenheim, "U.S. Subpoenas Block-Test Files in New Health Care Fraud Inquiry," *New York Times*, August 28, 1993, A1.

21. Castro, 38.

22. Ibid.

23. Ibid.

24. Barry Meier, "Doctors' Investments in Home Care Grow, Raising Fears of Ethical Swamp," *New York Times*, March 19, 1993, A14.

25. Ibid.

26. The restriction on medical services used by Medicare and Medicaid patients is necessary to avoid a 1991 rule issued by the Federal Department of Health and Human Resources.

27. Meier, A14.

28. Caryn Eve Murray, "Doc-u-Drama," *Newsday*,

April 13, 1993, 59; According to American Medical Association, no more than 30 of the nation's 126 accredited medical schools have such a program, either routinely or as a one-time trial project.

29. Barry Pierre-Pierre, "3d-World Medical Site: South Bronx," *New York Times*, May 4, 1993, B1.

CHAPTER EIGHT

1. William Lowther, "Medicare to the Rescue," *McLean's*, January 13, 1992, 32.

2. "Some Helpful Advice From Five Health Experts," *Money*, July 1991, 77.

3. Ibid.; According to a study published in the New England Journal of Medicine, nearly one of every ten health care dollars pays for nothing more than hospital paperwork; Francis Flaherty, "Paper Piles Up in Hospitals," *New York Times*, August 8, 1993, Business section, 2.

4. Marilyn Milloy, "Multiple Voices for Single Payer," *Newsday*, March 22, 1993, 15.

5. Philip R. Lee, and Richard D. Lamm, "Europe's Medical Model," *New York Times*, March 1, 1993, A15.

6. Roni Rabin, "'Free' System Has Its Price," *Newsday*, April 19, 1993, 22.

7. Ibid.

8. Ibid.

9. Philip J. Hilts, "Canada Is Found to Lead U.W. in Holding Drug Prices Down," *New York Times*, February 22, 1993, A10.

10. Robert Pear, "Clinton Aides Seek New Review Board for Drug Pricing," *New York Times*, May 17, 1993, A1.

11. Hilts, A10.

12. Survey jointly conducted by the *Wall Street Journal* and NBC News; Lowther, 32.

13. Rabin, 22.

14. Clyde H. Farnsworth, "Now Patients Are Paying Amid Canadian Cutbacks," *New York Times*, March 7, 1993, A1.

15. Ibid.

16. Ibid.

17. Glenn Kessler, "Bitter Medicine," *Newsday*, April 11, 1993, 45.

18. Rabin, 22.

19. Ibid.

20. Ibid.

CHAPTER NINE

1. Milt Freudenheim, "Making Health Plans Prove Their Worth," *New York Times*, August 8, 1993, 5.

2. Milt Freudenheim, "The Xerox Health-Care Model," *New York Times*, February 16, 1993, D1.

3. Larry Rohter, "Florida Blazes Trail to a New Health-Care System," *New York Times*, April 4, 1993, sec. 1, 1.

4. Robert Reinhold, "Wrestling Health-Care Costs to the Mat," *New York Times*, February 10, 1993, A1.

5. Peter Kerr, "Changes Would Transform Worlds of Doctors, Hospitals, and Insurers," *New York Times*, September 11, 1993, 10.

INDEX

ABOUT THE AUTHOR

Nancy Levitin is a graduate of the New York University School of Law and a member of the bars of New York and New Jersey. She has counseled and represented elderly and disabled clients in connection with health care planning and needs. As a freelance writer, Nancy Levitin, like her mother, Gilda Berger, writes well researched and judicious books on controversial and complex subjects.